i am a
DISCIPLE

=== A 40-Day Student Discipleship Journal ===

THIS BOOK BELONGS TO:

Grace Koehler

deep
DISCIPLESHIP

LeaderTreks
YOUTH MINISTRY

MAKING DISCIPLES. DEVELOPING LEADERS.

I Am a Disciple: A 40-Day Student Discipleship Journal

Copyright © 2014, 2017, 2018, 2020 by LeaderTreks

ISBN 978-1-939031-19-8

Published by LeaderTreks
25W560 Geneva Road, Suite 30
Carol Stream, IL 60188

leadertreks.org
877-502-0699

i am a
DISCIPLE

A 40-Day Student Discipleship Journal

TABLE OF CONTENTS

Outreach

Worship

Apologetics

Community

Appendix

Have you ever noticed that people who do the same thing often look alike? Soccer players spend hours running outside. When they practice, they get weird tan lines from their shin guards, and their legs are powerful from the running and kicking. Swimmers look the same, too. Their shoulders are chiseled, while their hair is often tinted from the chlorine.

The funny thing is, before a swimmer takes swim lessons or a soccer player joins a team, they don't look like those in the group. Their muscles haven't started shaping the same way from all the drills yet. They haven't gotten their farmer's tans from spending hours in the sun. It takes a while before they get in a groove and learn where they need to be on the soccer field, or in what order they should swim the relay. But eventually they start to look alike. They learn their group's slang, start to finish each other's sentences, and laugh at the inside jokes.

It works like this when we follow Christ, too. To be a disciple of Christ means to follow him. We learn from him. We do what he does, go where he goes, and think about what he thinks about. Eventually we start getting on the same page as him, and our communication syncs up. We adopt his rallying cry and mission statement. And the farther we go down the road with Christ, the more we start to look like him. We find ourselves responding to situations the way he would. Our spiritual muscles strengthen as we walk the same terrain that he walked.

—— HOW IT WORKS: ——

This book is designed to help you walk the road behind Jesus. It will take you through some of the core things that he taught his 12 disciples when he was walking the earth 2,000 years ago. It's designed to equip you to follow Christ by developing some of the spiritual muscles you'll need to make the journey.

In this journal, you'll encounter challenges, hard questions, and Bible studies, all of which focus on EIGHT CORE ROOTS OF DISCIPLESHIP. At the end of each chapter, you'll find a MENTOR PAGE. This page is designed for you to use in relationship with an adult who is farther down the discipleship road than you.

(If you don't have a mentor, ask your youth pastor or some other trusted adult the best way to go about finding one.) Each day is different than the last and no two days are the same, so no matter how you're wired there will be something for you!

Throughout this journal, you'll also find the **MARKS OF A DISCIPLE**. These are things that Christ-followers are committed to and have in common, like connecting with God through prayer, applying his Word to our lives, serving without personal agendas, managing God's gifts, and many other things.

For he has rescued us from the dominion of darkness and brought us into the kingdom of the Son he loves, in whom we have redemption, the forgiveness of sins.

— Col. 1:13-14

This is how God showed his love among us: He sent his one and only Son into the world that we might live through him.

— 1 John 4:9

Rescue —
Chapter 1

DAY 1 - *Lost*

Take a journey back to a time when you were six years old. Imagine you are at a store with your mom. You stop and look at a toy for a moment, and when you look up, she's gone. Your stomach churns and panic sets in: *Where did she go? What if I never find her? I'm lost!*

That terror in a six-year-old heart rings true in our lives today, but on a much larger scale. Not only are we lost; we're also slaves. We're held captive to sin—you know, doing things we know are wrong but just can't stop, like hurting others, hurting ourselves, and hurting God. We need a rescuer to save us from our slavery. There's only one person who can do just that: Jesus. God loved us so much he sent Jesus to rescue us from sin's grasp and bring us freedom. He even invited us to join the mission to show others the way to true freedom as well.

Read Luke 15:1–8, and use the 5P method to study this passage.

PURPOSE
Why do you think Jesus used this parable? Why is it important enough to be in the Bible? In a sentence or two, write what you think the overall theme or topic is.

Jesus used this Parable to show the Pharisees how important his children are to him. This is showing the Lords immeasurable love, and he'll take the time for everyone.

PRIMARY VERSE
Which verse seems to contain the most important thought in the passage? Which one stands out to you? Write it out. This quote is also saying that heaven watches + rejoices

"In the same way, there is more joy in heaven over one lost sinner who repents and returns to God than over 99 others who are righteous and haven't strayed away"!

PROMISES
Make a list of any promises you find in this passage.

1. He won't leave us behind
2. He values everyone (sinners + the rightous

PROBLEMS
If you find anything you don't understand—even if it's just a word—write it down as a question. Then ask someone for the answer or look it up yourself.

No not really

PRACTICAL APPLICATION
What do you need to change or work on so that what you've read is real in your life? Be specific—your application should tell who, what, and when.

★ I need to rejoce for fellow christans
★ I need to trust that God is out looking for m

DAY 2 - Stockholm Syndrome

In 1973 Janne Olsson, on leave from prison, attempted to rob a bank in Stockholm, Sweden. When two police officers went in, Olsson shot one, and then he took four bank employees hostage. Through negotiations he got his friend to join him, and they held the hostages in a bank vault for six days— threatening to kill them several times.

But during the standoff, the victims became attached to their jailers. At one point, they even rejected help from officials. After they were released, some even defended their captors. Psychologists call this "Stockholm syndrome." Why would people defend someone who imprisoned them? It sounds crazy, right?

Oddly enough, we are just like them. We are slaves to sin, and we can't escape it on our own. But we often act just like those bank employees. We're hurt by sin, but we start to make excuses for it: "It's not that bad. Maybe it won't hurt as much next time." Instead of turning to Jesus, we try to find ways to cope with our imprisonment—success, sports, popularity, relationships, or empty religion—but none of those things bring freedom. The only way to escape this prison is to be rescued.

The following verses walk us through the way to salvation in Christ. Read through them, and then reflect on how Jesus broke into your life and brought you to freedom:

ROMANS 3:23
For all have sinned and fall short of the glory of God.

ROMANS 6:23
For the wages of sin is death, but the gift of God is eternal life in Christ Jesus our Lord.

ROMANS 5:8

But God demonstrates his own love for us in this: While we were still sinners, Christ died for us.

ROMANS 10:9–10

If you declare with your mouth, "Jesus is Lord," and believe in your heart that God raised him from the dead, you will be saved. For it is with your heart that you believe and are justified, and it is with your mouth that you profess your faith and are saved.

EPHESIANS 2:8–9

For it is by grace you have been saved, through faith—and this is not from your-selves, it is the gift of God—not by works, so that no one can boast.

WHEN DID YOU FIRST REALIZE THAT BEING A GOOD PERSON WASN'T ENOUGH? HOW DID YOU RECOGNIZE YOU WERE LOST AND IN NEED OF RESCUE? To be honest I haven't really been a good person, I aknowladge that I need help but I don't want to give up certian things.

WHO HAS BEEN INFLUENTIAL IN SHOWING YOU CHRIST AND WHAT IT MEANS TO BE A CHRIST FOLLOWER? HOW DID THEY DO THIS? I think aubrey loftis has such a good work ethic and has put in the time to work on her faith & I want to be more like her

WHAT DOES IT MEAN TO DECLARE, "JESUS IS LORD"? WHAT DOES THAT LOOK LIKE IN YOUR DAILY LIFE? HOW HAVE YOU DONE THAT IN THE PAST? That means surrender yourself. I have never been willing to, but I've hit rock bottom.

DAY 3 - The Weight of Sin

DEPRESSION, FAMILY DESTRUCTION, **perfectionism,** BULLYING, INSECURITIES, fear of the future, **EATING DISORDERS, rejection,** SELF DESTRUCTIVE HABITS, **disappointment, HOPELESSNESS,** LACK OF PURPOSE, feelings of worthlessness, **apathy,** LONELINESS, FEELING ABANDONED, **ANXIETY,** selfishness, **pride,** hate, **DESPAIR,** idolatry, **greed,** GOSSIP

Today is going to be hard. You're going to take some time to reflect on where you've been and the effect sin has had on your life. The dark places sin takes us can be devastating. Sometimes we make choices that drive us further and further from God. Sometimes our darkest place is the result of someone else's sin, but it sends us into a spiral of our own sin. In order to go forward, we have to know where we've been. God's grace in our lives is seen more clearly and joyously when we remember what we've been saved from. It's like the stars. We can only see them shine in the midst of a dark night.

Step away from all distractions. Turn off your phone. Get away from the TV and computer. If you can, take a walk to get away from the demands around you. Take some time to pray before you get started.

List the top three struggles you have faced from the list above. If you need to, add your own struggles.

1. Lying
2. sexuality
3. porn addiction

Describe the situations surrounding each of these three struggles.

1. I'm struggling with lying because I want to cater/please every

2. Idk I think I'm positive with who I am, but my prnt

3. Porn addiction started in like 7th grade

What emotions did you experience during those times? How did they affect your actions?

1. Anger

2. Lust

3. depression

Draw a symbol that represents what you were going through in the midst of each of these issues. You may have one symbol that ties all three together or three different symbols. Jot down a few words to explain your symbol(s).

→ A mess/tornado because that's how I feel

How has Jesus rescued you from these struggles? How is your life different since you encountered Christ?

Tbh I haven't felt Christ yet

Draw a symbol or picture of who you now are in Christ. Write a few words to explain your symbol.

→ my heart is beging to be clean

Marks Of A Disciple

Disciples of Christ recognize their NEED for a Savior. (Romans 3:23)

Yesterday was a heavy day. It's often painful to remember the darkness that we lived in before Christ. But it does remind us of the unbelievable grace that is poured out on us. Christ rescued us from the muck of our lives and gave us true freedom. But after that, we shouldn't just stand around doing a happy dance, content because we are so blessed. He invites us to join in his mission. We have the opportunity to point others to the only one who can **truly** save them. Jesus came to seek and save the lost (Luke 19:10), and in John 20:21 he says, "Peace be with you! As the Father has sent me, I am sending you."

He calls us to a new life that demonstrates the radical **transformation** that comes with a relationship with Christ. Our lives are a proclamation of who Jesus is and what he has done. So we live radically because he lived radically. We care about the lost because he cared for them. We love like no other, we serve the servants, and we bind up the brokenhearted. We shout his message of freedom with our lives, and we declare his redemption with our lips. Are you ready to live out the mission?

Read 1 Peter 2:9–17 using the SPECK Bible study method. Think specifically about how this helps you join the great mission that Jesus has called you to on earth.

SINS TO AVOID

Make a list of any sins—wrong actions, attitudes or thoughts—mentioned in the passage.

① Thinking Lustfully towards others

② lying

PROMISES TO CLAIM

Make a list of the promises in this passage. Promises give us confidence when we doubt God or face difficult times.

① Earth isn't our home ② we are his chosen one's ③ we are his instruments and he greatly rejoce

EXAMPLES TO FOLLOW

What examples do you find in the passage? Is there a right way of thinking or acting described in the passage that you should take as an example for your life?

① Live an exampery life ② Respect Authorty ③ Treat everyone ④ Love your Spuritul family ⑤ Respect the with dignity Goverment

COMMANDS TO OBEY

Write out all the commands you find. If a passage encourages you to take a certain action, take it as a command and write it down.

KNOWLEDGE OF GOD TO APPLY

What does the passage tell you about God that you can apply to your daily life? God's character shines throughout Scripture.

we can see that God has a plan, + is watching over us

Disciples of Christ SPREAD THE WORD
of Christ's story with others. (Mark 16:15)

DAY 5 - Shine a Light on Sin

In the book *The Count of Monte Cristo*, Edmund Dantes is betrayed and unjustly imprisoned in the worst dungeon in France, the Château d'if. He spends 14 years sleeping on the cold stone ground of his cell. Edmund escapes and recovers his friend's treasure, elevating him to a life of luxury. He lives in a mansion with a plush bed. One day his servant walks in and finds Edmund sleeping on the floor. Edmund has a lavish bed to sleep in any time he wants, but he keeps going back to his old way of life.

Similarly, Jesus has rescued us from the prison of sin. Yet sometimes the lure of our old life draws us back. It's like we've had the shackles of sin taken off, but we go back and put our wrists in them again because they're familiar.

When those old sins creep back into our lives, it's easy to get discouraged. We can feel frustrated with ourselves and overwhelmed by shame. During those times, we have to go back to the truth that Christ proclaimed when he rescued us: we are children of God. This sin doesn't make us any less God's children, but it does get in the way of our relationship with him. So how do we deal with it?

To escape the quicksand of shame, we have to take time to evaluate our lives regularly, recognize sin that is growing within, and bring it to God. James 5:16 says, "Therefore confess your sins to each other and pray for each other so that you may be healed." We're going to do just that.

1. ASK GOD TO REVEAL YOUR SINS TO YOU—THE DEEP, UNDERLYING, SUBTLE SINS THAT OTHERS MIGHT NOT NOTICE. WRITE OUT THE SINS THAT COME TO YOU.

2. HAVE YOU WRONGED SOMEONE? GO TO THEM AND ASK FOR FORGIVENESS. IT'S EASY TO LOSE YOUR RESOLVE, SO DON'T HESITATE.

3. NOW CHOOSE A CHRIST-FOLLOWER YOU RESPECT AND TRUST, SOMEONE YOU CAN SHARE YOUR OTHER STRUGGLES WITH (A CLOSE FRIEND OR MENTOR). CONFESS YOUR SIN TO THAT PERSON AND TO GOD. TAKE SOME TIME TO PRAY WITH THEM FOR HEALING. IT MAY BE DIFFICULT TO LET SOMEONE ELSE SEE YOUR SIN, BUT IT'S AN IMPORTANT STEP IN LEAVING YOUR SIN BEHIND, ONCE AND FOR ALL.

"It is fitting, that by the confession of our own wretchedness, we show forth the goodness and mercy of our God, among ourselves and before the whole world." — John Calvin[1]

MENTOR PAGE - Rescue

This page is designed for you to use in relationship with a mentor. If you don't have a mentor, skip it for now, but seriously consider finding one. Start by praying, and then ask someone (like a youth worker) to recommend a person who would be a good fit. Or if you know someone with a deep faith and the kind of character traits and faith you want to develop, ask them to mentor you. Most people will be more than thrilled and truly honored to mentor someone.

Questions to go through with your mentor:

1. What's your rescue story? Think through what you wrote on Day 2 about how Jesus became your Savior. What was that process like?
2. How do you deal with sin in your life? After we become Christ-followers, sin doesn't have the power over our lives that it did before we knew Christ, but it's still a daily reality. So how do you deal with it? Or if you aren't at that stage yet, how do you want to deal with it?
3. Take a look at the symbols or drawings you made on Day 3. Explain them to your mentor. Why did you choose those symbols? Is there a difference between the symbols you chose? If so, what changed?
4. On Days 1 and 4 you made some very specific life applications. Share those with your mentor. Did you follow through on them? Do you need someone to keep you accountable?

Until your next meeting:
Take a minute to figure out when you and your mentor will get together next.
My mentor and I will meet: _____ (when) at _____ (where).

Are there any specific ways your mentor can pray for you until then?

Since the children have flesh and blood,
he too shared in their humanity so that
by his death he might break the power of
him who holds the power of death—that
is, the devil—and free those who all their
lives were held in slavery by their fear
of death.
— Heb. 2:14-15

"Jesus came to announce to us that an identity based on success, popularity and power is a false identity— an illusion! Loudly and clearly he says: 'You are not what the world makes you; but you are children of God." — Henri Nouwen[2]

"Don't let the noise of others' opinions drown out your own inner voice."
— Steve Jobs[3]

Identity —
Chapter 2

DAY 1 - Who am I?

"Who am I?" Have you ever asked yourself that? On your first day of middle or high school, did you think through how you would reinvent your identity, making sure to leave the bad pieces behind? Think about going through the first steps of filling out your profile on a social media account. It starts off with simple, straight-forward questions like age and gender. But then it goes deeper, and you find yourself trying to sum up your whole identity in fewer than 100 words.

When we answer these questions for a public audience, we sometimes fudge the truth. We may embellish some of our skills and interests or only share the trendy things about us to fit in with friends or to impress a crush.

This is similar to the concept of a yearbook photo—only one snapshot in time, yet it summarizes an entire year. When you're in college looking back, will that one photo remind you of who you were at that age? It doesn't include the three different clothing trends that came in and out of style, different hairstyles, friends, and break-ups. You only get one outfit, one hairstyle, and hopefully a smile. You can choose to give an accurate representation of yourself, or you can dress differently on picture day—just in case someone you like checks it out.

The world has a lot of places to discover and question our identities. But have you ever wondered what God has to say about your identity?

This week we will explore what God's Word says about identity. It just might challenge what you write in your "About Me" section.

Think about how you want others to see you and how you'd like to portray yourself. How closely does that line up with who you really are?

What would you write in your "About Me" section at this exact moment?

How do you feel your current identity measures up to the identity of a fully devoted Christ follower?

Do you know the identity God has given you? Explain what you think that is.

DAY 2 - Two Identities

Sometimes answering the question "Who am I?" can be difficult because we have an inner conflict. Who we want to be clashes with who we really are.

Have you ever noticed that when you're around certain friends you might start to act like them, but when you're around your family you act completely different? It's almost like you have a closet of different personalities, and you're trying on a different one for each situation.

The book of Genesis explains how God created Adam, but God didn't just give him a name and a physical body; he gave him an identity. Adam was given a purpose from the very beginning: he was placed in authority over the animals and named each one. He was told to be a leader, and he was told to be creative. God knew that Adam wasn't meant to be alone. He needed a helper. That is all part of Adam's identity from the first few chapters of the Bible.

We later see Adam struggle with an inner conflict. After Adam and Eve gave in to temptation and sinned, their identity became twisted. They were like the evil twins of who God created them to be. Their children were born with this twisted identity, and so were we. Thanks to Jesus' death and resurrection, God's forgiveness allows us to take on a redeemed identity. But the conflict between our sinner's identity and our redeemed identity never fully goes away in this life.

The New Testament is full of people struggling with this same battle. Today we are going to use the OPA method to discover the differences between the sinner's identity and the redeemed identity. This will help you understand Adam's inner conflict and hopefully shed light on your own.

Read Ephesians 2:1–10.

OBSERVATION

Compile all the facts found in these passages. Make several observations about what you read.

Sinner's Identity | **Redeemed Identity**

PRINCIPLES

Draw a few principles from the observations you made. What is God trying to teach you in these passages?

Sinner's Identity | **Redeemed Identity**

APPLICATION

How will you apply these principles to your life? Be specific—a good application will tell who, what, and when.

DAY 3 - Lies and Truths

Can you remember a time when someone called you a name? Or when someone told you that you were "no good at _____ ," or that you were "not (strong, smart, athletic, old) enough." The people love to set up systems that put others down, creating ways to bolster themselves at the cost of people around them. The world picks a label for you, and it sticks, whether you like it or not. It's rare for someone to overcome the identity the world gives you.

Misty Copeland is a good example of that. She was told she was too short, too old, and had the wrong body type for ballet. But she didn't care what they said. Misty didn't accept that as her identity. She poured time and sweat into ballet and went on to become the third African-American female soloist and first African-American female principal dancer in the American Ballet Theater's history. Her story is unusual, so rare that Under Armor has used her story to create a 15 million dollar campaign for their women's clothing, starring Misty. Her commercial went viral and gained over 4 million views in the first week. As Christ-followers, we get to take this one step further than Misty.

Once we reject the identity the world has given us, we can claim the identity of God's children. In order to root yourself in the identity Christ gave you, start by recognizing the lies and truths about your identity.

WRITE DOWN THE LIES THE WORLD HAS TOLD YOU ABOUT WHO YOU ARE.

WRITE DOWN THE TRUTHS OTHERS HAVE TOLD YOU ABOUT WHO YOU ARE.

Find time this week to complete this challenge and write down your thoughts.

Go back through your list of lies you've heard about yourself. Think of one that hurts the most and remember who told it to you. WHY DID IT HURT SO MUCH? WHY ARE YOU STILL LETTING IT TAKE A HOLD OF YOU?

Paul tells us to take off our old self and put on the new self. Imagine yourself wearing this lie and allowing it to dictate how you view your identity. Now imagine taking that lie off and burning it to ashes. HOW WOULD THIS CHANGE YOUR IDENTITY? HOW CAN YOU KEEP THAT LIE FROM BECOMING A PART OF WHO YOU ARE?

To learn more about Misty Copeland, check out this article: time.com/3083114/misty-copeland-under-ar-mour-i-will-what-i-want/.

DAY 4 – *Spiritual Gifts*

As Christ-followers, not only do we have a redeemed identity as God's children, but we also are equipped with everything we need to follow Christ and live on his mission. God gives us spiritual gifts that are an important part of our identity as Christ-followers. These are special abilities and talents that all Christ-followers have. But we don't all have the same spiritual gifts. Our gifts were chosen to fit our specific passions and role in the work God is doing in the world.

Turn to page 122 in the Appendix, and you'll have a chance to take a Spiritual Gifts Assessment to identify some of the clues in your life that show what your spiritual gifts may be. Keep a couple things in mind when you take this assessment:

1. Go with your gut. When you are answer these questions, usually your gut reaction best reveals who you truly are. When we think too long about an answer, we start to think about how we want to answer the question instead of what is the truest answer.

2. When you're done taking the assessment, find your top gifts on the following pages, and read about where they are described in the Bible, how they are used on a team, and what some of the potential pitfalls are when we misuse them.

MY SPIRITUAL GIFTS ARE:

Disciples of Christ use their
SPIRITUAL GIFTS to bless
the church. (1 Corinthians 12:7)

"If one member suffers, all suffer together;
if one member is honored, all rejoice together.
Now you are the body of Christ
and individually members of it."
— I Corinthians 12:26,27 (ESV)

DAY 5 – *Transformation*

You've had a lot of time to think about your identity this week. You had the opportunity to discover your spiritual gifts, examine the lies that have been told to you by this world, looked at the difference between a sinner's identity and a redeemed identity, and hopefully started to understand who God created you to be.

Now look back to Day 1 of this week. What did you **write down** for your "About Me" section? It's possible that you would change some of what you wrote then because God is starting to change the way you see yourself. Maybe you are forming a tighter grip on your redeemed identity as God's child.

There is a great story in the Bible from a former **Christ-hater** named Saul (also called Paul) who experienced just that. He had a radical **transformation** from sinner to Christ-follower. Many of the letters he wrote to early churches discuss how God used his past to reach the lost while he lived in his new identity.

Read Acts 9:1–19 and Acts 11:25–27. Follow the 5P study method and see how Saul takes off his old identity and puts on his new redeemed identity.

PURPOSE
WHY DO YOU THINK THE AUTHOR WROTE THIS? WHY IS IT IMPORTANT ENOUGH TO BE IN THE BIBLE? In a sentence or two, write what you think the overall theme or topic is.

PRIMARY VERSE
WHICH VERSE SEEMS TO CONTAIN THE MOST IMPORTANT THOUGHT IN THE PASSAGE? WHICH ONE STANDS OUT THE MOST TO YOU? Write it out.

PROMISES
MAKE A LIST OF ANY PROMISES YOU FIND.

PROBLEMS
IF YOU FIND ANYTHING YOU DON'T UNDERSTAND—EVEN IF IT'S JUST A WORD—WRITE IT DOWN AS A QUESTION. Then ask someone for the answer or look it up yourself.

PRACTICAL APPLICATION
WHAT DO YOU NEED TO CHANGE OR WORK ON SO THAT WHAT YOU HAVE READ IS REAL IN YOUR LIFE? Be specific—your application should tell who, what, and when.

Disciples of Christ follow **GOD'S MISSION** for their lives. **(Proverbs 3:5–6)**

MENTOR PAGE - Identity

Questions to go through with your mentor:

1. What did you write in your "About Me" section from Day 1?
2. What's the difference between your identity with Christ (your redeemed identity), and your identity before Christ (your sinner's identity)?
3. What are some of lies you believed (or maybe still believe) about your identity? How do you overcome those lies?
4. What are your spiritual gifts? How are you using them now? How can you grow in them and use them more in the future?
5. On Days 2 and 5 you made some very specific life applications. Share those with your mentor. Did you follow through on them? Do you need someone to keep you accountable?

Until your next meeting:
Take a minute to figure out when you and your mentor will get together next.
My mentor and I will meet: _____ (when) at _____ (where).

Are there any specific ways your mentor can pray for you until then?

"You were taught, with regard to your former way of life, to put off your old self, which is being corrupted by its deceitful desires; to be made new in the attitude of your minds; and to put on the new self, created to be like God in true righteousness and holiness."

— Eph. 4:22-24

"Once you become aware that the main business that you are here for is to know God, most of life's problems fall into place of their own accord."
— J.I. Packer[4]

"My trust in God flows out of the experience of his loving me, day in and day out, whether the day is stormy or fair, whether I'm sick or in good health, whether I'm in a state of grace or disgrace. He comes to me where I live and loves me as I am."
— Brennan Manning[5]

Knowledge — Chapter 3

DAY 1 - Why Know God?

Think about your best friend. How much time have you invested in that friendship? How many conversations? Texts? Meals? The truth is, your friendship probably takes a lot of work. It probably eats up a lot of your days, forcing you to drive out of your way, making you listen to the same stories twice, and causing you to compromise on which movie you'll see on Friday night. Friends cost a lot when you think about it. But they're also worth it, aren't they? After all, no one knows you like your best friend. Who else can you just be yourself around? No one is as fun to hang out with or as good a sounding board when you've had a bad day.

Our relationship with God should be similar. Sure, it costs something. It takes an investment of time and a sacrifice of your priorities. But just like your best friend, it's worth it.

God wants that deep relationship with you even more than your best friend. He doesn't want you to just know about him, memorizing facts from Sunday school. He doesn't want you to know a twisted version of himself that some people will try to sell you. He wants you to actually know him, to have conversations with him, watch his miracles, trust him, and experience his presence. When you get to know God, your life will never be the same.

Take a few minutes to go through this list of names and descriptions of God. Think through your own life, and circle the ones that you have experienced or have encountered first-hand.

- Refuge – Isaiah 25:4
- Rock – Deuteronomy 32:4
- Holy – Psalm 99:9
- Love – 1 John 4:8
- Unchanging – James 1:17
- Creator – Genesis 1:1
- Forgiving – Psalm 86:5

- Compassionate – Daniel 9:9
- Merciful – James 5:11
- Patient – Psalm 86:15
- Truth – John 14:6
- All Powerful – Jeremiah 32:17
- Always Present – Psalm 139:7
- All Knowing – 1 John 3:20
- Good – Psalm 25:8
- Just – 2 Thessalonians 1:6
- Defender of the weak – Psalm 82:3
- Savior – 1 John 4:14
- Comforter – Jeremiah 8:18
- Deliverer – Romans 11:26
- Great Shepherd – Hebrews 13:20
- Guide – Psalm 48:14
- Light of the World – John 8:12
- King of Kings – 1 Timothy 6:15
- Father – Romans 8:15

NOW DESCRIBE THREE TIMES WHEN YOU SAW ONE OF THESE CHARACTERISTICS FIRST-HAND.

For example:
I KNOW GOD IS MIGHTY BECAUSE I HAVE SEEN THE REDWOODS IN CALIFORNIA, AND KNOW THAT ONLY A MIGHTY GOD COULD CREATE THAT.

DAY 2 - How to Know God

"How do we know God is real?" That's a question we've all asked at one point or another. Frankly, it's a good question.

1. God shows himself to the world in many ways. God reveals himself in nature, in people, and in our daily lives. Have you ever looked at the sky, or stood on a mountain and thought, *This has to have been made by God?*

Today, find a quiet spot (outside if you can), and put away all distractions, like your phone. Answer the following question in the space provided.

As you look around, in what ways does God reveal himself through his creation? These are the whispers of God—stuff that sort of hangs out in the background of our lives that we usually ignore.

1.   6.

2.   7.

3.   8.

4.   9.

5.   10.

2. God also shows himself to us when he works supernaturally in creation. These are miracles—the kind of things that, were they to happen in front of you, would force you to rub your eyes to make sure you weren't hallucinating—like when Jesus healed the blind and the sick.

3. Finally, God shows who he is through the words and events recorded in the Bible. The apostle Paul describes Scripture as "God-breathed" (2 Tim. 3:16). In a special way, God actually wrote it, using a bunch of people over many, many years.

In 2 Timothy, Paul wrote to Timothy from prison, urging him to stick with Scripture and let it teach him. Paul had been mentoring Timothy, and since Paul was about to be executed, he used this last letter to Timothy to pass on the greatest knowledge he had—to always return to the Bible for wisdom and strength.

Read 2 Timothy 3:12–17. Choose one of the Bible study methods you've used so far (5P, SPECK, or OPA) to study this passage. You can find an example of the 5P method on page 10–11, the SPECK method on page 16–17, and the OPA method on page 26–27.

Disciples of Christ LISTEN to the Bible's message. (Romans 15:4)

Prayer is one of the most powerful tools we have to build our relationship with God, but often it goes overlooked. To many of us, prayer is an inconvenience before a meal, or a last-ditch effort before a test. But how often do we think of prayer as a way to get to *know* God?

When you pray, is it a one-way monologue or a two-way conversation? Do you stop to think about who he is and how that relates to who you are? Prayer doesn't have to be formal or pretentious. You don't have to have all the words right. God isn't interested in "perfect" prayers, he prefers authentic prayers—the kind that expose our hearts.

It's this conversation—this friendship—that pleases God. (People like Moses and Abraham are good examples of this.) And it can happen anywhere and anytime. Build this friendship by carving out some intentional time to pray, not just when it's convenient. You might also find it helpful to take a walk around your neighborhood or in a park as you pray. Or maybe you could turn the radio off whenever you're in the car and spend that time talking to God.

For the next week, try keeping a prayer journal. That may sound complicated, but it's really just writing out your prayers instead of saying them in your head. Use the following questions from the ACTS prayer method to guide your thoughts, and write down your prayers every day this week. (Check in the back of this book for pages where you can do this.) One cool thing about writing down your prayers—you can go back to them later to see how God has answered them.

Use this ACTS prayer model each time you pray this week:

1. Adoration: Praise God for who he is. What fact or characteristic about God makes you glad?

2. Confession: Humble yourself. If Jesus took a tour of your heart right now, what would he find?

3. Thanksgiving: Be grateful. What happened in your life today that you can thank God for?

4. Supplication: Tell God your needs. Where do you need him to work in your life?

5. Listen: What is God saying to you? Think about things others have told you, past experiences, familiar Bible passages, and even the Holy Spirit's tugging on your heart. God speaks through these things.

Disciples of Christ CONNECT with God through prayer. (Psalm 145:18)

DAY 4 - God is Trinity

Water is pretty sweet if you think about it. It exists in three states: solid, liquid, and gas. Imagine a cup of ice water. It holds the liquid (water), solid (ice cubes), and gas (in the air above the water) all at the same time. It's not hard to grasp how that works, because we can see it.

The Trinity, on the other hand, is much harder to understand. God is three persons at once: the Father, the Son (Jesus Christ), and the Holy Spirit. The Trinity isn't three separate gods, but it's also not one God who changes from one person into another. It can be pretty confusing to understand how one God can be three persons at once, all the time. **We know the truth of this from the Bible, but how it all works together is somewhat mysterious since God is huge and we are pretty small.**

We saw the relationship between the Father and the Son in the Rescue chapter at the beginning of this book: the Father loves us and sent his Son, Jesus, to rescue us from sin. But the Holy Spirit is often overlooked and undervalued—mostly because it's hard to explain who the Holy Spirit is.

In the Old Testament, the Holy Spirit only came to visit people for a time, empowering kings and prophets to do God's work. But when Jesus came down to Earth, died for us, and went back up to heaven, he sent the Holy Spirit to be with us forever, saying the Spirit would act as our "advocate." An advocate is someone who works or argues for the cause of another person.

The Holy Spirit convicts us, prays for us when we don't have the words, and allows us to connect to Jesus and the Father in incredible ways. Make no mistake, the Holy Spirit is a person, not a force or an "it." The Holy Spirit is completely God, just like the Father and the Son.

WHY DO YOU THINK JESUS FELT IT WAS SO IMPORTANT TO SEND THE HOLY SPIRIT WHEN HE WENT BACK UP TO HEAVEN? (TAKE A LOOK AT ACTS 1:7-8.)

JOHN 3:8 DESCRIBES THE HOLY SPIRIT LIKE THE WIND. YOU CAN'T SEE THE WIND, BUT YOU CAN FEEL IT. HAVE YOU EXPERIENCED OR SEEN EVIDENCE OF THE HOLY SPIRIT AT WORK IN YOUR LIFE? WHEN?

HOW ARE THE DIFFERENT STATES OF WATER LIKE THE THREE PERSONS OF THE TRINITY? HOW DO THEY FALL SHORT IN EX-PLAINING THE TRINITY?

Have you ever wanted something so badly that you did something kind of crazy to get it? We all have things we are so passionate about that it seems hard to imagine letting any obstacles get in our way.

Zacchaeus knew that feeling well. He was an outcast—a tax collector, someone who no one enjoyed seeing because he was usually at their door to take their money. As a matter of fact, he probably took more than they actually needed to give. Tax collectors had a habit of over-collecting and keeping the extra money for themselves. So as you can imagine, he wasn't a popular guy.

But he'd heard about Jesus, and something about the way Jesus talked about life and God sparked his interest. So he embarrassed himself by climbing a tree in order to listen to his words. Imagine bringing stilts to hear the President speak at a fancy dinner so you could see over everyone else—not exactly a good social move.

When Jesus saw Zacchaues, he looked past what society thought of him and saw Zacchaues for who he really was: a lost soul in need of a Savior. He told Zacchaues the he was going to his house for dinner that night, breaking all kinds of social rules. And Zacchaues was so moved by the love of Jesus that he volunteered to give half of his wealth to the poor and pay back anyone he'd overcharged four times the amount he took!

Are you pursuing God as passionately as Zacchaues did? Read the story of Zacchaues in Luke 19:1–10, and then use the OPA method to respond.

OBSERVATION

Compile all the facts found in the passage. Make 20 to 30 observations about what you read.

PRINCIPLES

Draw a few principles from the observations you made. What is God trying to teach you in this passage?

APPLICATION

How will you apply these principles to your life? Be specific—a good application will tell who, what, and when.

MENTOR PAGE - *Knowledge of God*

Questions to go through with your mentor:

1. What characteristics of God (from Day 1) did you circle? Tell your mentor about the times you experienced them.
2. How important is the Bible in your life? Why?
3. Do you find it easy or hard to talk with God? Do you prefer to pray alone or in front of other people? Why?
4. How have you seen the Holy Spirit at work in your life? Do you have any questions about the Trinity (God the Father, Son, and Holy Spirit)?
5. How are you pursuing God?
6. On Days 2 and 5 you made some very specific life applications. Share those with your mentor. Did you follow through on them? Do you need someone to keep you accountable?

Until your next meeting:
Take a minute to figure out when you and your mentor will get together next.
My mentor and I will meet: _____ (when) at _____ (where).

Are there any specific ways your mentor can pray for you until then?

"The heavens declare the glory of God;
the skies proclaim the work of
his hands. Day after day they pour
forth speech; night after night they
reveal knowledge. They have no speech,
they use no words; no sound is heard from
them. Yet their voice goes out into all
the earth, their words to the ends of
the world." — Ps. 19:1-4

"If we only had eyes to see and ears to hear and wits to understand, we would know that the Kingdom of God in the sense of holiness, goodness, beauty is as close as breathing and is crying out to be born both within ourselves and within the world." — Frederick Buechner[6]

"What you do in the present—by painting, preaching, singing, sewing, praying, teaching, building hospitals, digging wells, campaigning for justice, writing poems, caring for the needy, loving your neighbor as yourself—will last into God's future. ... They are part of what we may call building for God's kingdom."
— N.T. Wright[7]

Kingdom —
Chapter 4

DAY 1 - *Something Deeper*

Do you ever get the sense that there's more to the world than what you can see? We love movies where a bland piece of furniture contains a portal to Narnia and schools for super powered prodigies hide in plain sight. And while these stories may seem far-fetched, they kind of ring true. The world we encounter every day feels a little too superficial to be all there is.

That's one of the beauties of Scripture. It gives you a peek behind the curtain, a glimpse into the supernatural activity of God. In Luke 17:20–21, Jesus says, "The coming of the kingdom of God is not something that can be observed, nor will people say, 'Here it is,' or 'There it is,' because the kingdom of God is in your midst." In other words, the kingdom of God isn't just a future paradise waiting for us when we die—it's all around us right now. As Christ-followers, we actually live in the kingdom of God right now, but it isn't obvious if you don't know it's there.

The best part? The supernatural reality of God's kingdom makes our everyday lives even more significant. It adds depth and weight to our actions and decisions. Every person is more valuable than we could possibly imagine. The daily choices we make have eternal consequences. But like eyes adjusting to the bright morning light, we have to practice seeing our world in the context of God's kingdom.

IS THERE ANYTHING ABOUT THE WAY THE WORLD WORKS THAT DOESN'T SEEM QUITE RIGHT? Do you feel in your gut that some things should be different? If so, list them below.

In God's kingdom, people are precious. The God of the universe created them (in his image) and longs to embrace them in his family. List three ways you would treat people differently if you lived according to this kingdom reality.

1.

2.

3.

God's kingdom also shows us that the choices we make have eternal significance. List three choices you made last week, and describe how they may have had a bigger impact than you realized.

1.

2.

3.

Now that we know there's something supernatural behind the curtain of everyday life, we can ask the question, What exactly is this kingdom of God? Is it a place we can go to? A code of rules we have to follow? An invisible reality we could see if we put on our x-ray glasses? It's all in the name. What makes something a *kingdom*? A king. The kingdom of God is all about Christ's rule. Unlike the kingdoms of the world, God's kingdom doesn't have borders. It exists anywhere and everywhere Christ is proclaimed as king.

So what kind of king is Christ? If we know something about our ruler, we'll learn more about the kingdom, itself—its laws, its people, its purpose. Thankfully, the Bible tells us about Christ's kingship. Long before Jesus was even born, God spoke through the prophet Isaiah, telling us what kind of king Jesus would be.

Read Isaiah 9:6-7, using the 5P method to study this passage.

PURPOSE
Why do you think the author wrote this? Why is it important enough to be in the Bible? In a sentence or two, write what you think the overall theme or topic is.

PRIMARY LINES
Which line or two seem to contain the most important thought in the passage? Which lines stand out to you? Write out these lines completely, underlining key words.

PROMISES

Make a list of any promises you find.

PROBLEMS

If you find anything you don't understand—even if it's just a word—write it down as a question. Then ask someone for the answer or look it up yourself.

PRACTICAL APPLICATION

What do you need to change or work on so that what you've read is real in your life? Be specific—your application should tell who, what, and when.

DAY 3 - Citizenship

Just like countries around the world today, the ancient Roman Empire granted citizenship to many of the people living in its territory. Whenever the Romans conquered a new area, the people of that land were automatically made citizens of Rome. Why? Because it turned them from adversaries into allies. It made them part of the group that cared about each other and the future of Rome. It's like a Kickstarter fundraiser. The minute you contribute to a campaign, you care way more about the product than you did before because now you've "bought in."

Unity
While there are major differences between citizenship in the kingdom of God and citizenship anywhere else, there are also some important similarities. Citizens of God's kingdom are united to each other, too. Whatever your differences before you became a citizen of the kingdom—race, wealth, politics, gender—you are now one with each other in Christ (Gal. 3:28). Because you've "bought in" to Christ's kingship, you're now equals, called to care for the people he loves.

Describe a time when you felt like you were part of a group, when you were accepted by others as an equal. WHAT WAS IT THAT MADE YOU FEEL THAT WAY?

HAVE YOU EVER HAD A DISAGREEMENT WITH A REALLY GOOD FRIEND? HOW DID YOU WORK THROUGH THAT OR OVERCOME IT SO THAT YOU COULD REMAIN FRIENDS?

SHOULD THE KINGDOM OF GOD BE FILLED WITH PEOPLE WHO ARE ALL ALIKE? WHY OR WHY NOT?

Privileges

Roman citizens were given a number of privileges non-citizens didn't have. For example, citizens of Rome could vote, own property, get married, and have a legal trial. Citizens of God's kingdom have privileges, too. We are guaranteed a personal relationship with God because we are adopted into his family; eternal life in his presence, starting now; and a future without suffering, pain, or sadness after Christ's return. Our sins are wiped clean, and we are freed from the power of Satan and sin.

WHAT ARE SOME OF THE PRIVILEGES YOU RECEIVE FOR BEING A CITIZEN OF YOUR OWN COUNTRY? List them below.

LIST THE PRIVILEGES AND GIFTS YOU RECEIVE AS A CITIZEN OF THE KINGDOM OF GOD (think back to the Rescue and Identity chapters in this book). Next to each privilege, explain why it's important to you.

DAY 4 - *The Kingdom Way*

Like all kingdoms, God's kingdom has a set of values for its citizens to live by. But these values aren't what you'd expect. The following story will help explain.

A resident assistant (RA) on a college dorm floor knew he had a great group of guys. Most were on the soccer team, so they already knew and looked out for each other. But this group was also pretty creative when it came to pushing the boundaries. When the RA returned to the dorm one night, he discovered that an incredible game of "soccer" had broken out in the hallway. It was elaborate, with point systems based on what door you hit and where you hit it. The guys were having a blast. There was only one problem: the three giant windows outlining the lounge were taking some hits. The RA thought through his options and went to grab a dry erase marker. Without saying a word, he began writing on one of the lounge windows:

Lounge windows: $480.
Soccer in the hall: Priceless.

He could have instituted more rules, shut down the game, or yelled. After all, there were consequences to breaking the windows, but there was also permission to have a blast, be creative, and make memories.

Like this creative game of soccer, God's kingdom doesn't follow the world's normal set of rules: survival of the fittest, more money means more power, and get revenge to get ahead. It has a different value system, a higher one. In the kingdom, the least are the greatest, the last are first, and the humble are honored. The world's rules have a cost to them, one you will never recoup. But the kingdom of God is priceless.

Read Matthew 5:3–12. This list of kingdom values is called the Beatitudes. Use the OPA method to study this passage.

OBSERVATION

Compile all the facts found in these passages. Write down observations about what you read.

PRINCIPLES

Draw a few principles from the observations you made. What is God trying to teach you in these passages?

APPLICATION

How will you apply these principles to your life? Be specific—a good application will tell who, what, and when.

Disciples of Christ respond in THANKFULNESS to God's many gifts. (1 Thessalonians 5:18)

Today, you'll practice living out the value system of **God's kingdom** you learned about yesterday. Pick one item from each of the following five categories and commit to doing it at some point in the next few days. If you're looking for a real challenge, pick two items from each category. Check off each item once you've accomplished it.

The Last Shall Be First

❏ Let someone else cut in front of you in line.

❏ Open the door for people behind you and let them through first.

❏ While driving in bad traffic, let one more car merge in front of you than you normally would.

❏ If you have younger siblings, do something you wouldn't normally do to serve them.

Forgiveness vs. Revenge

❏ Go out of your way to encourage someone who has wronged you in the past.

❏ If you play a sport, go one whole game without taking revenge on another player.

❏ Do your best work on an assignment for the teacher you like the least.

❏ Go one entire lunch with your friends without gossiping about anyone.

Flashy vs. Meek

❏ Get ready one morning without using a mirror.

❏ Pick one achievement (in school, sports, music, etc.) and commit to not bragging about it to anyone.

❏ Go one entire lunch without talking about yourself.

❏ Do one act of service that no one knows about.

Comfort vs. Service

- ❏ Trade an afternoon of streaming shows for serving somewhere outside your own home.
- ❏ Do an extra chore for your parents or siblings without being asked.
- ❏ Offer to pray for someone you wouldn't normally pray with.
- ❏ Ask your parents or a pastor about how you can serve a community in need. Then do it!

Horading vs. Sacrifice

- ❏ Spend some time collecting things you don't use, and give them away to Goodwill, a thrift store, or your church.
- ❏ Give money when your church collects the offering this week.
- ❏ Give the money you'd normally spend on Starbucks, fast food, or something else you don't really need to someone who needs it more.
- ❏ Take time you'd normally spend on yourself and use it to teach someone else something (e.g., teach a sibling a basketball move, tutor a neighborhood kid, or help a friend struggling in class).

"But seek first the kingdom of God and his righteousness, and all these things will be added to you." — Matt. 6:33, ESV

Disciples of Christ SERVE wholeheartedly without a personal agenda. (1 John 3:18)

MENTOR PAGE – Kingdom

Questions to go through with your mentor:

1. In which areas of your life is Jesus your King? In which areas of your life are you king?
2. In your own words, describe what it means to be a citizen of the kingdom of God.
3. Who has been an influential person in your faith story? How has that person shown Jesus to you?
4. What are some of your daily decisions that have an impact in the kingdom of God?
5. On Days 2 and 4 you made some very specific life applications. Share those with your mentor. Did you follow through on them? Do you need someone to keep you accountable?

Until your next meeting:
Take a minute to figure out when you and your mentor will get together next.
My mentor and I will meet: _____ (when) at _____ (where).

Are there any specific ways your mentor can pray for you until then?

"Jesus answered him, 'Truly, truly,
I say to you, unless one is born
again he cannot see the kingdom
of God.'" — John 3:3, ESV

"Have you no wish for others to be saved? Then you're not saved yourself. Be sure of that." — Charles H. Spurgeon[8]

"We are most in line with the Spirit, most faithfully obedient, when instead of trying to manipulate people into faith, we simply live in that freedom and let the Spirit do the work of transformation." — Mark Galli[9]

Outreach —
Chapter 5

DAY 1 – Go

> "THEREFORE GO AND MAKE DISCIPLES of all nations, baptizing them in the name of the Father and of the Son and of the Holy Spirit, AND TEACHING THEM TO OBEY EVERYTHING I HAVE COMMANDED YOU. And surely I am with you always, to the very end of the age."
> (MATTHEW 28:19-20).

Think back to when you got your first cell phone. (If you haven't yet, imagine the day you will.) Once you got the phone out of the box and turned it on, what was the first thing you did? My guess is that you shared the good news with someone. You either called or texted a friend to let them know about your latest gadget and gave them your number.

Our normal response when we receive something great is to show it to others. We want everyone to know about it because we are proud and excited. So why should our faith in God and our gift of salvation be any different? Jesus' last words to his disciples were about just that. He commanded the disciples to share the message that he had been teaching them—not only by telling others the truth, but also by living it out. Sharing your faith requires both words and actions.

This week we are going to examine what it means to share our faith with others. Did you know that the Great Commission in Matthew 28 is not the first time Jesus commanded the disciples to go? In Matthew 10, he gave them more detailed instructions with some guidelines on how to do it.

Let's take a deeper look into Jesus' instructions in Matthew 10 using the OPA method. See how he commanded the disciples to "go" and how it applies to you.

Read Matthew 10:1-20.

OBSERVATION

Compile all the facts found in the passage. Make several observations about what you read.

PRINCIPLES

Draw a few principles from the observations you made. WHAT IS GOD TRYING TO TEACH YOU IN THIS PASSAGE?

APPLICATION

HOW WILL YOU APPLY THESE PRINCIPLES TO YOUR LIFE? Be specific —a good application will tell who, what, and when.

DAY 2 - The Lost and the Least

Yesterday you did a Bible study in Matthew 10. In verse 6, Jesus tells them to "Go to the lost sheep." Jesus wanted his disciples to go to the lost, the overlooked, those who were wandering and didn't have an opportunity to hear the good news any other way.

In Matthew 25:40, Jesus talks about another group of people who are overlooked: the least. He is referring to people with deep needs, like food, clothes, and a place to live. He is also referring to the sick and those in prison. They are cast aside, lonely, and hurting.

How often do we share with people in our close circle of friends, but avoid the lost and the least? Jesus didn't come to save just our friends and family. He came for everyone. His wants us to share with the lost and the least because we may be the only ones who will.

Who are the lost and the least in your life? Maybe there is a group of people at school or in your community who are overlooked. I bet you can think of someone who everyone else avoids or excludes.

Your challenge this week is to recognize one or two individuals each day who fit into these categories (the lost and the least). Fill in the space on the next page, as you find them. They might be on the news, walking by you on the street, someone on your Friends List, or someone in your church group. The first step to sharing with them is recognizing who they are. At the end of each day, pray for the people you wrote down. Take it one step further and find a way to encourage one person on the list before the week is over.

THE LOST

THE LEAST

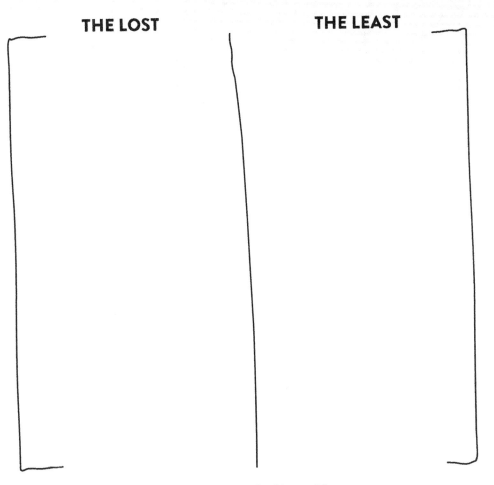

How will you encourage one of these people this week?

Disciples of Christ LOVE OTHERS as more valuable than themselves. (Philippians 2:3)

DAY 3 - A Light in the Dark

Jesus had a heart for the lost and least, and he often found himself going against the grain because of it—ridiculed for his interactions with them. Now that you have started recognizing the lost and least in your life, you can grow in compassion and get a glimpse of why Jesus went after them so passionately.

It's important to know that in Jesus' interactions with the lost and least, he developed close relationships with them without engaging in their sinful behavior. He had to remain a light in a dark place. That's a big challenge, but it's important when reaching out.

Read: Mark 2:13–17 and use the 5P method to discover how Jesus reached out to the lost and least.

PURPOSE
Why do you think the author wrote this? Why is it important enough to be in the Bible? In a sentence or two, write what you think the overall theme or topic is.

PRIMARY VERSE
Which verse seems to contain the most important thought in the passage? Which one stands out most to you? Write it out.

PROMISES
Make a list of any promises you find in the passage.

PROBLEMS
If you find anything you don't understand—even if it's just a word—write it down as a question. Then ask someone for the answer or look it up yourself.

PRACTICAL APPLICATION
What do you need to change or work on so that what you have read is real in your life? Be specific—your application should tell who, what, and when.

Disciples of Christ show EVIDENCE of faith through fruit of the Spirit. (Galatians 5:22–23)

DAY 4 - Make It Personal

Let's be honest, sharing your faith with others can be terrifying. It often takes us right out of our comfort zones and drops us in unfamiliar territory. What are we supposed to say? What if we don't know all the answers to questions they might ask us? What if they reject us altogether? Jesus didn't give the disciples all the answers before sending them out. He knew they would still have questions, and so will we. When God tells us to reach out to the lost, it's not because we have perfect biblical knowledge. It's because God equipped us in other, unique ways. He has provided you with the words, the relationship, the personal experience, and the other distinctive qualities that may be exactly what the other person needs to hear.

Who originally shared their faith with you? Your parents? A friend? A stranger? What did they say to you? Did they know all the answers? Many times, sharing the good news of Christ comes from our own experiences and personal faith stories.

Today we are going to brainstorm some of the influential times in your own life when people shared their faith with you. Take some time to answer and reflect on the questions below.

HAS A STRANGER EVER SHARED JESUS WITH YOU? WHAT DID THEY SHARE? HOW DID IT MAKE YOU FEEL?

HAVE YOU EVER HAD SOMEONE OFFER TO PRAY OVER YOU WHEN YOU DIDN'T ASK FOR IT? HOW DID THAT MAKE YOU FEEL?

DO YOU REMEMBER A TIME WHEN SOMEONE YOU KNEW WELL SHARED JESUS WITH YOU? WHAT DID THEY SHARE? HOW DID IT MAKE YOU FEEL?

HAS ANYONE EVER GONE OUT OF THEIR WAY TO SERVE YOU OR HELP YOU FOR NO REASON EXCEPT TO SHOW YOU CHRIST'S LOVE? WHAT WAS SIGNIFICANT ABOUT THAT EXPERIENCE?

HAS SOMEONE SHARED A PERSONAL STORY WITH YOU THAT HELPED YOU WHILE YOU WERE GOING THROUGH A DIFFICULT SITUATION? IF SO, HOW DID THEIR STORY HELP YOU DEAL WITH THE SITUATION?

DAY 5 - *Your Faith Story*

Jesus came to tell the world about God and to fulfill the rescue plan God had put in place. And we're invited into that rescue plan, **too**. Jesus came to train and equip us to share his good news. Have you ever wondered why you and I don't go to heaven the minute we acknowledge Jesus as Lord of our lives? It's because God's plan for rescuing the world includes us! We're supposed to spread the word, to reach into the hard to find places, the areas of people's lives that no one else is willing to touch, and to share Jesus' love. We're supposed to seek out the lost, the least, the untouchables, and bring them into God's family. When he had one last opportunity to speak to his followers, he commanded them to go and share his message.

Reaching out to those around us doesn't come naturally to everyone. We have to practice and prepare so we will know what to say when the time comes. 1 Peter 3:15 says, "Always be prepared to give an answer to everyone who asks you to give the reason for the hope that you have. But do this with gentleness and respect."

Part of your purpose in the world is spreading Jesus' story. Often the easiest place to begin is by sharing your own faith journey. Take a few minutes to think about and write out some key parts of your faith story.

How has knowing Jesus changed your life?

Write down a few milestone moments in your faith. Maybe you went from knowing to believing or had a breakthrough in your understanding of Jesus.

In your own words, why did Jesus come to die for us? How does that make a difference in your everyday life?

What does a relationship with Christ look like?

How does someone follow Jesus? (Go back to Day 2 in the Rescue chapter for some key Bible verses about this.)

Disciples of Christ can SHARE their faith story. (1 Peter 3:15)

MENTOR PAGE – Outreach

Questions to go through with your mentor:

1. How easy or hard is it for you to share your faith? Why do you think that is?
2. On Day 2, you made a list of the lost and the least you've seen around you. Who did you decide to encourage? How did you encourage them?
3. Who has been an influential person in your faith story? How has that person shown Jesus to you?
4. How did you answer the question from Day 5, *What does a relationship with Christ look like?*
5. On Days 1 and 3, you made some very specific life applications. Share those with your mentor. Did you follow through on them? Do you need someone to keep you accountable?

Until your next meeting:

Take a minute to figure out when you and your mentor will get together next.

My mentor and I will meet: _____ (when) at _____ (where).

Are there any specific ways your mentor can pray for you until then?

"My sheep wandered over all the
mountains and on every high hill. They
were scattered over the whole earth,
and no one searched or looked for them."
— Ezek. 34:6

"For we are God's handiwork, created in Christ Jesus to do good works, which God prepared in advance for us to do." — Eph. 2:10

———— — ————

"The more you pray, the less you'll panic. The more you worship, the less you worry. You'll feel more patient and less pressured." — Rick Warren[10]

Worship —
Chapter 6

DAY 1 - What is Worship?

IF YOU HAD TO EXPLAIN WORSHIP TO A YOUNGER SIBLING, HOW WOULD YOU DESCRIBE IT?

WHAT ARE WORSHIP PASTORS USUALLY IN CHARGE OF?

Many of us have been trained to believe that worship only happens on Sunday mornings. The *worship* pastor leads us to sing *worship* songs during the *worship* service. But after the service is over, we don't jump into our *worship* car to drive to our *worship* house and eat our *worship* lunch. For some reason, worship stays behind, locked in the church building like leftovers we'll reheat in a week.

So, what IS worship? Worship is an all-the-time-thing. Take a look at Psalm 71:6, 8: "I will ever praise you. ... My mouth is filled with your praise, declaring your splendor all day long." That doesn't mean you have to sing praise songs nonstop. But you should live every part of your life to glorify God—loving him and the people he loves, thanking him, and following his direction for your life.

What is NOT worship? In Isaiah 29:13, God's prophet tells God's people why their worship just isn't cutting it: "The Lord says: 'These people come near to me with their mouth and honor me with their lips, but their hearts are far from me. Their worship of me is based on merely human rules they have been taught.'" In other words, if we sing all the right songs and raise our hands at the right times, but live the rest of our lives with our hearts far from God, we aren't really worshipping.

AFTER LEARNING A LITTLE BIT ABOUT WHAT WORSHIP IS AND ISN'T, HAS YOUR DEFINITION OF WORSHIP CHANGED AT ALL? IF SO, HOW? IF NOT, DO YOU THINK MOST PEOPLE HAVE THE CORRECT UNDERSTANDING OF WORSHIP? WHY OR WHY NOT?

IS THERE ANYTHING ELSE IN YOUR LIFE THAT YOU WORSHIP—THAT YOU GIVE MOST OF YOUR TIME OR THAT YOUR HEART CARES ABOUT MORE THAN GOD (SUCCESS, COMFORT, BEING RIGHT ALL THE TIME, A CRUSH OR SIGNIFICANT OTHER, OR EVEN YOURSELF)?

DAY 2 - *Obedience is Worship*

Have you ever disobeyed your parents? Maybe you **stayed out too late**, watched that movie you weren't supposed to, or something **worse**. Now, put yourself in your parents' shoes. How do you think they felt about it?

Many times, we do the same thing with God. In John **14**, Jesus tells us that if we love him, we will obey his commands. But how many **times do we end up following** our own rules, instead? "Just this once ..." we say, and **we ignore God's commands** so we can do what feels good in the moment.

In this passage, Jesus outlines a pretty radical view **of obedience**—shaping your life after his. You may have heard the saying that "imitation is the sincerest form of flattery." Well, in this case, that's true! By acting **like Jesus**, we honor him and show him love.

Being obedient, imitating Jesus, and following his will—these things can be really tough on our own. Thankfully, God has given us his Holy Spirit to help us out. The Spirit will never leave us, and he will help us obey God **even when it's hard.**

Read John 14:8–21. Use the OPA method to study **this passage.**

Disciples of Christ LOVE GOD by obeying him in all circumstances. (John 14:15)

OBSERVATION

Compile all the facts found in the passage. Make 20 observations about what you read.

PRINCIPLES

Draw a few principles from the observations that you have made. What is God trying to teach you in this passage?

APPLICATION

How will you apply these principles to your life? Be specific—a good application will tell who, what, and when.

DAY 3 - *Arrow Prayers*

It's all too easy to go about life without thinking much about God. Sure, you remember he's there when you're at church or when you pray before a meal, but what about the rest of the time? You can't live a life dedicated to worship when most of the time your mind is far away from God. So how can we stay focused on him?

Think about it this way—say you have a physics test coming up in two weeks, and you don't know the material. You could cram all of the material over lunch the day of the test. But that probably won't work, and even if you ace the test, you'll forget everything the minute it's over. You're feeding your brain too much information over too little time. You'd be better off breaking the content into bite-size chunks to study as many times as possible over the full two weeks.

This same idea can help you go from thinking about God only once a week to worshipping him all day every day. One long prayer before dinner may be a good start, but it's like cramming before a test—it doesn't stick. Instead, try saying arrow prayers: super-short prayers you can "shoot up" to God whenever you need to remember he's there.

In Nehemiah 6:9, Nehemiah deals with a rough situation by shooting up an arrow prayer. His enemies are trying to convince him that he's too weak to do God's work, so he prays to God, "Now strengthen my hands." This is a great arrow prayer: short, simple, and connected to an immediate need.

Now it's your turn:

List three daily situations that might make good opportunities for arrow prayers (struggles, interactions, or things you're thankful for).

1.

2.

3.

Now write out three one-sentence arrow prayers for each situation you listed above. Try saying them each day this week, and see if you remember God's presence more than you did before.

1.

2.

3.

"So whether you eat or drink or whatever you do, do it all for the glory of God." — 1 Cor. 10:31

DAY 4 - A Lifestyle of Worship

Michael Phelps didn't become a record-breaking Olympic swimmer by simply showing up for the games and working hard for two weeks. He had to live the life of an Olympian for years before he actually competed. Similarly, worship is more than singing on the weekend—it is a lifestyle.

How we're made
Michael Phelps's body is made to swim. He has a six-foot, seven-inch wingspan so he can take longer strokes. His legs are short compared to his upper body, causing less resistance in the water. And his size-14, double-jointed feet act like flippers.

God has made each of us to worship (Isa. 43:6–7). Our individual talents and passions were given to us so we could do God's work in the world (Eph. 2:10).

HOW DID GOD CREATE ALL PEOPLE TO WORSHIP HIM?

HOW DID GOD CREATE YOU UNIQUELY TO GIVE HIM GLORY?

What we do
Phelps has an incredible work ethic. He trains in the pool six days per week and trains with weights three times a week. He regularly changes his exercises so his body won't adapt to any set routine.

In Romans 12:1–16, God calls us to be living sacrifices, to worship God by following his will. We should train ourselves (1 Cor. 9:24–27) to glorify God through everything we do.

IF YOU HAD A "WORSHIP WORKOUT ROUTINE," WHAT WOULD BE ON THAT LIST?

HOW COULD YOU TRANSFORM HUMDRUM ACTIVITIES LIKE CHORES OR MEALS INTO ACTS OF WORSHIP?

What we consume

Phelps eats an absurd amount of fat and calories to keep up with his training: three fried egg sandwiches, an omelet, a bowl of grits, three slices of French toast with powdered sugar, three chocolate chip pancakes, two cups of coffee—and that's just for breakfast!

We have to pay close attention to what we take in, too (not just food). First, we should avoid consuming garbage that leads to unhealthy worship (Eph. 5:18; Titus 3:9; 2 Tim. 2:14). Second, whatever we take in, we should do so in thankfulness (1 Cor. 10:31). Finally, we can't forget the health food—God's Word is like food meant to nourish us (Jer. 15:16).

WHAT IS THE "JUNK FOOD" IN YOUR WORSHIP LIFE?

OTHER THAN THE BIBLE, WHAT ARE "HEALTH FOODS" THAT HELP FUEL A LIFESTYLE OF WORSHIP?

More about Michael Phelps's rigorous routine can be found here: www.bodybuilding.com/fun/michael-phelps-the-phenom.

Marks
Of A
Disciple

Disciples of Christ make time to REST, dedicating that time to God. (Genesis 2:3)

DAY 5 – Service is Worship

Jesus' brother describes worship in this way: "Religion that God our Father accepts as pure and faultless is this: to look after orphans and widows in their distress." (James 1:27)

According to James, when we serve others, we worship God. Remember what we said about imitation being the sincerest form of flattery in Day 2 of this week? When you worship God by helping those in need, you'll start looking a lot like him.

But not all service is worship! Are you doing it to pad a college application, because your parents are pushing you, or because you want people to think you're a great person? In those situations, you're serving others to serve yourself, not God.

How much do you look like Jesus? Do your actions and your service exhibit a life of worship? Or do they reveal someone focused only on themselves?

Take the following challenge:
This week, try doing 3 random acts of kindness. Think of it as service for ninjas—you're in, you're out, and the person you served never knows it was you. Do something that truly helps someone else, but be sneaky about it. Don't tell anyone about it before or after. When it's only known between you and God, you'll be more likely to see it as an act of worship, done to glorify God instead of yourself.

Fill out the chart on the next page to plan three random acts of service you could do this week. Remember, it's not about seeing the person's reaction so you can feel or look good; it's about worshipping God by serving the people he loves.

	Person to serve	Act of service	How I'll stay anonymous
Random Act of Kindness 1			
Random Act of Kindness 2			
Random Act of Kindness 3			

Disciples of Christ SACRIFICE their time, resources, and abilities. (Hebrews 13:16)

MENTOR PAGE - *Worship*

Questions to go through with your mentor:

1. Share with your mentor how you defined worship in Day 1.
2. How hard or easy is it to stay focused on God throughout your daily life? Why?
3. What were your arrow prayers this week? Why did you choose those three prayers?
4. When is it hardest to worship? When is it easiest to worship? Why?
5. On Day 2 you made some very specific life applications. Share those with your mentor. Did you follow through on them? Do you need someone to keep you accountable?

Until your next meeting:
Take a minute to figure out when you and your mentor will get together next.
My mentor and I will meet: _____ (when) *at* _____ (where).

Are there any specific ways your mentor can pray for you until then?

"The highest form of worship is the worship of unselfish Christian service. The greatest form of praise is the sound of consecrated feet seeking out the lost and helpless."
— Billy Graham[11]

"The greatest single cause of atheism in the world today is Christians who acknowledge Jesus with their lips and walk out the door and deny him by their lifestyle. That is what an unbelieving world simply finds unbelievable." — Brennan Manning[12]

"You never know how much you really believe anything until its truth or falsehood becomes a matter of life and death to you." — C.S. Lewis[13]

Apologetics —
Chapter 7

DAY 1 – I am the Truth

Imagine following your favorite celebrity around for a day, able to hear every conversation. You would see what they cared about, what they mumble under their breath, and what they believe. It's the same when we follow Christ. The Bible gives us access to even the little moments of his life, like prayers whispered, words spoken on the cross, and truths he desperately wanted his disciples to know. Learning about him is an important part of following him. It also helps us avoid falling for the lies our world tells us every single day.

Many people in our culture claim that all religions and belief systems teach the same doctrines, worship the same God, and lead us toward the same destiny. That sounds nice, doesn't it? It means we don't have to step on people's toes and that anyone can do anything and still get to heaven. The problem is, many of these religions teach opposing views of reality and truth. Can two opposite beliefs both be true? Of course not! To say something is true, we have to admit that opposing ideas are false.

As disciples of Christ, we believe that Jesus is "the way the truth and the life. No one comes to the Father except through [him]" (John 14:6). Jesus said these words and based his entire ministry around them. His disciples were so sure this was true that they gave their lives for it. No matter how nice it sounds to have many ways to God and eternal life, there's an infinite cost if they turn out to be untrue. And if we have the truth in our hands, we have a great responsibility to share it with the world, even if that world hates absolutes and loves relativism.

Take some time to reflect on the different belief systems you see around you by answering these questions.

WHAT DOES YOUR CLOSEST FRIEND BELIEVE ABOUT GOD? WHAT DO YOUR PARENTS BELIEVE? DO YOU KNOW WHAT YOUR FAVORITE CELEBRITY BELIEVES?

EVEN IF YOU BELIEVE THAT JESUS IS THE TRUTH, DO YOU THINK IT'S IMPORTANT FOR OTHER PEOPLE TO BELIEVE THE SAME THING? WHY OR WHY NOT?

HOW DOES MEDIA PORTRAY TRUTH? DOES IT AGREE THAT THERE'S ONE TRUTH, OR DOES IT ARGUE THAT WHAT EACH INDIVIDUAL BELIEVES ISN'T THAT IMPORTANT, AS LONG AS THEY GET ALONG?

HOW SHOULD THIS VERSE AFFECT YOUR LIFE: "But in your hearts revere Christ as Lord. Always be prepared to give an answer to everyone who asks you to give the reason for the hope that you have. But do this with gentleness and respect" (1 Pet. 3:15)?

DAY 2 - Hard Truth

Today we are going to look at what it means to be a **Christ-follower** in a world that claims many truths (or no truth at all). Jesus knew it wouldn't be easy for his disciples to follow him. That's why he said things like, "**Whoever** wants to be my disciple must deny themselves and take up their cross **daily** and follow me" (Luke 9:23). The truth was going to be hard for a lot of people to swallow, but that didn't make it any less true.

John, one of Jesus' close friends, wrote down a significant **conversation** that Jesus had with his followers when he knew his death on **the cross** was just around the corner. They had just finished what we call the Last **Supper**, and Jesus was telling his disciples the things that they absolutely *had* to know. Time was short, and Jesus needed them to understand some key truths. Jesus **needed** them to know how to stand as his disciples, even after he left them.

Read John 15:1–25 and use the 5P method to see how **these** same truths interact with our own lives.

PURPOSE
Why do you think the author wrote this? Why is it important enough to be in the Bible? In a sentence or two, write what you think the overall theme or topic is.

PRIMARY VERSE
Which verse seems to contain the most important thought in the passage? Which one stands out most to you? Write out.

PROMISES
Make a list of any promises you find in this passage.

PROBLEMS
If you find anything you don't understand—even if it's just a word—write it down as a question. Then ask someone for the answer or look it up yourself.

PRACTICAL APPLICATION
What do you need to change or work on so that what you have read is real in your life? Be specific—your application should tell who, what, and when.

Marks Of A Disciple

Disciples of Christ APPLY God's Word in their lives. (James 1:22)

It's normal to take common beliefs as facts—like when some well-meaning adult told you not to swallow gum because it would stay in your stomach for 7 years (not true). Who has the time to fact-check every little thing you hear? Yet sometimes these misconceptions can be harmful. Take the Bible, for instance. Many people think the Bible says things it doesn't, and when that happens, we twist the truth of God. As followers of Christ, we must eagerly seek out God's Word to know the truth so we can present it to the world.

Let's test your knowledge on a few biblical truths. Check T (true) or F (false) for each statement below. Then compare your answers to the key.

[T] [F] 1. God won't give you more than you can handle.

[T] [F] 2. "This, too, shall pass," is found in the Bible.

[T] [F] 3. Jesus never sinned.

[T] [F] 4. The Bible says, "Cleanliness is next to godliness."

[T] [F] 5. "God helps those who help themselves," is found in the Bible.

[T] [F] 6. The little drummer boy is not a part of the Christmas story in the Bible.

[T] [F] 7. All religions lead to the same truth, as long as they teach us to love.

[T] [F] 8. The Bible says, "Money is the root of all evil."

[T] [F] 9. What's true for one person may not be true for another.

[T] [F] 10. The Apostle Paul became all things to all men in order to spread the gospel of Jesus, but he never compromised the gospel.

Marks Of A Disciple

Disciples of Christ THINK about God's truth on a regular basis. (Philippians 4:8)

Did any of these answers surprise you?

Why is truth sometimes hard to accept? What makes something easier to believe?

How important is the Bible to a follower of Jesus?

ANSWER KEY

1. **F:** This is actually a reference to temptation, not burden. We won't be tempted to the point that we have to sin (1 Cor. 10:13), but the burdens of the world often push people to their breaking points. But we can find courage in the fact that God himself helps carry our burdens (Ps. 68:19).

2. **F:** This is actually a proverb from Persian poetry.

3. **T:** Jesus never sinned (2 Cor. 5:21). He was tempted (which is good news for us because he can really relate to us), but he never gave in to temptation (Heb. 4:15).

4. **F:** For some of us, this is good news. This phrase actually came from a Babylonian and Hebrew proverb brought to popularity by Sir Francis Bacon and John Wesley.

5. **F:** This is found nowhere in the Bible. Its origins go back to ancient Greece, and its modern English version is often attributed to Benjamin Franklin and Algernon Sidney.

6. **T:** Even though the little drummer boy shows up in many Christmas songs and images, he never actually appeared in the Bible at the birth of Jesus.

7. **F:** Remember from Day 2 of this week, Jesus is the only way (John 14:6). The major world religions teach surprisingly different things about God (or gods, or no deity at all).

8. **F:** The verse many people are thinking of actually says the root of all evil is "the love of money," not money itself (1 Tim. 6:10). It's a subtle difference, but significant.

9. **F:** Truth is absolute (John 14:6, Heb. 13:8-9). Regardless of how positive, negative, fair, or unfair it seems, the truth is still true.

10. **T:** This is from 1 Corinthians 9. Paul worked hard to bring the gospel of Jesus to many different kinds of people in many different situations. He was a master at reaching out.

DAY 4 - Truth in Love

When it comes to being a disciple of Christ, knowing the truth is incredibly important—especially because we'll face resistance, persecution, and even hate because of it. But we can't just bash people over the head with truth. We must communicate it with love.

Paul wrote a letter to people living in a city called Ephesus to encourage them in as Christ followers. The first part of this letter, which we call the book of Ephesians, focuses on God's mercy, love, and grace to us. One main focus in the second half of the letter is the importance of living by the truth of God with love as its foundation. As you read this section of Scripture, keep in mind the question, Why is love so important when living and speaking truth to others?

Read Ephesians 4:14–29 and use the OPA method to study this passage.

OBSERVATION

Compile all the facts found in the passage. Make several observations about what you read.

PRINCIPLES

Draw a few principles from the observations you made. What is God trying to teach you in this passage?

APPLICATION

How will you apply these principles to your life? Be specific—a good application will tell who, what, and when.

DAY 5 - The Truth about Me

Have you ever thought about who others *think* you are, versus who you actually are? There's a lot of reasons for this—maybe they haven't spent time with you, maybe you've never shown them your true self, or maybe they assume they know you because of a stereotype or because they know your family. Either way, there can be a big difference between who others think you are and who you truly are.

Today you're going to explore that difference by drawing out (yes, stick figures are okay) 5 "truths" that others think about you, and then drawing out the real truth about you. Here's an example of one high school student:

HIGH SCHOOL STUDENT

Who my mom thinks I am.

Who my dad thinks I am.

Who my best friend thinks I am.

Who my teacher thinks I am.

Who my youth pastor thinks I am.

Who I actually am.

Why do you think the way other people see you often seems so different from the way you see yourself?

Do you ever find yourself becoming a different person in different situations? Why?

Now it's time to draw your own. First, fill in your own name as the title and then write down five different people or social groups you're around a lot (friends, parents, youth leader, youth group, grandparents, siblings, teachers, crush, significant other).

Next, draw a picture or write a description of how each person/group perceives you. Finally, in the last box titled "Who I actually am," be honest with yourself and draw a picture or write about who you really are.

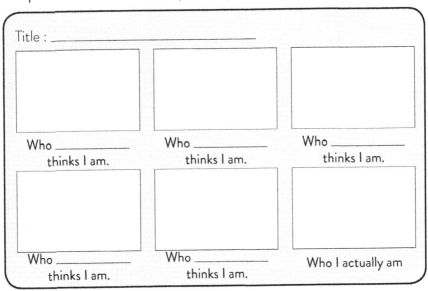

Are you proud of how you appear in each picture? Why or why not?

What is something you wish you could change about **how you present yourself to the world?**

Would you change anything about who you really are?

Now let's draw out how you can intentionally show **God's truth** to each of the groups you put in the boxes you just created. How can **you use your** actions and words to show God's truth with love? Look back at **the Scriptures** in this chapter (and those from the Outreach chapter) to influence **your drawings.**

Title : _____

How I can show God's truth to_____.	How I can show God's truth to_____.	How I can show God's truth to_____.
How I can show God's truth to_____.	How I can show God's truth to_____.	How I can keep God's truth in my own heart.

MENTOR PAGE - Apologetics:

Questions to go through with your mentor:

1. How does biblical truth affect your daily life?
2. How do you decipher what is true or what isn't true?
3. How do you react when people question your faith or God's truth?
4. Share your meme from Day 5 with your mentor. What did you find surprising about the differences between the truth about you and how others perceive you?
5. On Days 2 and 4 you made some very specific life applications. Share those with your mentor. Did you follow through on them? Do you need someone to keep you accountable?

Until your next meeting:
Take a minute to figure out when you and your mentor will get together next.
My mentor and I will meet: _____ (when) *at* _____ (where).

Are there any specific ways your mentor can pray for you until then?

"What should young people do with their lives today? Many things, obviously. But the most daring thing is to create stable communities in which the terrible disease of loneliness can be cured."
— Kurt Vonnegut[14]

———— - ————

"How good and pleasant it is when God's people live together in unity!" — Ps. 133:1

Community —
Chapter 8

DAY 1 - What Is Community?

Have you ever been stuck at a friend's house for one too many nights? Maybe your parents were out of town so you had to stay there for an extended period of time. You probably went from doing most things on your own to doing *everything* with another person. By the end of your stay, you were likely begging to get some time to yourself.

Sometimes you need that alone time and personal space, especially if you're an introvert. But too much alone time can be just as bad—like when summer vacation starts out great, but after a few days you miss seeing your friends.

Did you know we were not created to be alone? When God made everything, including Adam, he said it was good. Yet he also said, "It is not good for the man to be alone," (Gen. 2:18; that's where Eve came in). Why do you think that is? Do you think we need other people just to keep us from getting lonely, or do you think there is something more behind it? This week we will explore why and how community is a part of following Jesus.

Take a few moments to think about the community and relationships in your own life by answering these questions.

HAVE YOU EVER BEEN ALONE FOR TOO LONG? HOW DID THAT FEEL?

WHEN YOU HAVE THE CHOICE DO YOU GRAVITATE TOWARD SPENDING TIME WITH OTHERS OR SPENDING TIME ALONE?

WHY DO YOU THINK GOD DIDN'T WANT ADAM TO BE ALONE?

WHAT DOES COMMUNITY LOOK LIKE IN YOUR CHURCH? NAME A FEW OF THE GROUPS YOU WOULD CONSIDER YOUR COMMUNITIES.

WHAT DO YOU THINK ARE THE MOST IMPORTANT INGREDIENTS FOR COMMUNITY?

Just like you were born into a family, we as Christ-followers are part of God's family. Here on earth we call that the church. It's not just the building you go to or your denomination, but the body of all Christ-followers everywhere.

When life is good, you may not have a strong desire for community. Real community almost seems like a hassle. But think back to a time when things were bad—end-of-the-world bad. Maybe you found out your parents were getting a divorce, a friend or family member passed away, or everything that could go wrong did go wrong on the same day. Imagine not having anyone to talk with, to encourage you, to pray with you and lighten your burden, just a bit.

Even Jesus, who was perfect, didn't do life alone. He called 12 men, all with different backgrounds and personalities, to become his community. They did everything together, supported one another, and encouraged each other. That does not mean they always got along—their different perspectives often clashed. Jesus spent years teaching the disciples about God, but whether they knew it or not, he was also teaching them about community. He showed them by example how to live together to honor God.

After Jesus died on the cross for our sins and rose up to heaven, his disciples were empowered to continue his work by spreading the word and making more disciples. They started what we now call the early church. Today, we are going to discover what community looked like to them.

Read Acts 2:41–47. Choose one of the Bible study methods you've used so far (5P, SPECK, or OPA) to study this passage. You can find an example of the 5P method on page 10–11, the SPECK method on page 16–17, and the OPA method on page 26–27.

DAY 3 - Authentic Community

Being a part of a community is more than being surrounded by people or having a position on a team or group. Many people are part of several groups but are still lonely, because the depth of their community is shallow.

The thing is, to follow Christ, to join his mission of making disciples and reaching the lost and the least of this world, we need some serious help. We need a ton of abilities, gifts, talents, resources, and wisdom. Thankfully, God already knew that! He set up the church to be a community where Christ-followers could get together, worship him, and do great things. The people who make up Christ's church should help each other out, rely on each other, and reach the corners of the world with the story of Jesus. Unfortunately, many of us have downgraded church to just the place we go on Sundays.

Take some time to evaluate your own community. Write down 5-10 names (maybe the ones in your small group or youth group) in the circles below according to the depth of your relationship.

1. FACE: You know their name, but you don't really know them.

2. FACTS: You know a little bit about them, where they live, what they like, what their family is like.

3. FEELINGS: You know about their opinions, how they feel about certain subjects, events, and a little bit of their story.

4. FEARS: Once you get to an authentic level of friendship, people begin to share their deepest concerns, their fears, and their anxieties. They start taking off the mask so you can see the real person beneath.

5. FAITH: This is the deepest level of friendship. You know about their walk with God; their temptations; their weaknesses; and their spiritual gifts, goals, and passions.

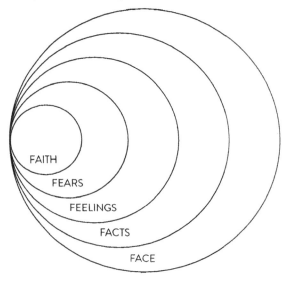

Now answer the following questions.

What's the deepest level of friendship you have with someone? Describe how your friendship progressed all the way to that level.

What level are most of your friendships on? Do you wish they were deeper? Why or why not?

How can you start moving your shallower friendships to deeper levels?

Disciples of Christ form DEEP RELATIONSHIPS with other disciples. (Hebrews 10:24–25)

DAY 4 – Community Lifestyle

On Day 2, we got a small picture of community in the early church. More than likely, if we were transported back in time to live for one week in the early church community, we would never want to come back. That's not to say those people were perfect. But the early church seemed to realize that life wasn't about them; it was about God and others. They saw each other's needs because they were focused outside of themselves. Imagine if that was your perspective the next time you went to the store to buy clothes. Would you concentrate on how m uch you could spend, or how much you could save to give away? Or imagine looking at Friday night with that perspective. Would you squeeze as much hangout time in as possible, or would you go out of your way to give your younger sibling a ride?

We are going to look at Romans 12:1–8 using the SPECK Bible study method.

SINS TO AVOID

Make a list of any sins—wrong actions, attitudes, or thoughts—mentioned in the passage.

PROMISES TO CLAIM

Make a list of the promises in this passage. Promises give us confidence when we doubt God or face difficult times.

EXAMPLES TO FOLLOW

What examples do you find in the passage? Is there a right way of thinking or acting described in the passage that you should take as an example for your life?

COMMANDS TO OBEY

Write out all the commands you find. If a passage encourages you to take a certain action, take it as a command and write it down.

KNOWLEDGE OF GOD TO APPLY

What does the passage tell you about God that you can apply to your daily life? God's character shines throughout the Bible as an example for us.

Disciples of Christ MANAGE their gifts to be used in God's kingdom. (1 Peter 4:10)

DAY 5 - What Is a Mentor?

One of the awesome things about the church is that people of all ages are available to influence our lives. We can look behind us and help the younger kids grow and learn to love Jesus—they look up to older students like you. We can also look around us and get some practical advice from our peers with different backgrounds. But one of the most crucial pieces of community is having a mentor who is farther down the road than us, someone who can walk with us through the good and bad times.

Mentors are like spiritual coaches. They have a larger perspective on life because they've been in your shoes and made it through. Do you have a mentor in your church community? Most of us look up to someone, but we don't reap the benefits of their knowledge and experience because we don't let them know we want their guidance (which most mentors are honored to give).

This week challenge yourself to look around at people in your church community to find a formal mentor—maybe a small group leader, another volunteer, or even a coach. Ask this person to be your mentor! Use the mentor pages at the end of each of these chapters to guide your meetings and conversations with your mentor.

If you already have a mentor, then focus on the question at the top of the next page to decide what areas you really want to focus on as you meet together in the future.

Name two or three adults who would make good spiritual mentors. WHY DID YOU PICK THEM?

WRITE DOWN TWO OR THREE AREAS IN WHICH YOU WANT TO GROW. Maybe you are struggling with temptation, want a deeper understanding of the Bible, or want to grow in a specific talent or gift.

HOW OFTEN DO YOU WANT TO MEET WITH ONE OF THESE PO-TENTIAL MENTORS? WHEN DO YOU PLAN ON ASKING THEM TO BE YOUR MENTOR?

Keeping these answers in mind, plan to ask one of these people to be your mentor and share with them the area you want to grow in, why you chose them, and how you think they could help. If the first person doesn't have time, don't get discouraged. Just ask the next person on your list from the first question.

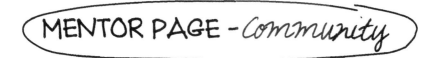

MENTOR PAGE - *Community*

Questions to go through with your mentor:

1. Do you have real, authentic community with other Christ-followers? Why or why not?
2. On Day 3, did you put anyone in the Level 5 circle of the diagram? Why or why not?
3. The early church was great at focusing on God and others. What takes up most of the focus in your life?
4. Share the areas of growth you wrote down on Day 5 so you can work on them with your mentor.
5. On Days 2 and 4 you made some very specific life applications. Share those with your mentor. Did you follow through on them? Do you need someone to keep you accountable?

Until your next meeting:
Take a minute to figure out when you and your mentor will get together next.
My mentor and I will meet: _____ (when) at _____ (where).

Are there any specific ways your mentor can pray for you until then?

"Live in harmony with one another. Do not be proud, but be willing to associate with people of low position. Do not be conceited." — Rom. 12:16

YOU'RE DONE!

... with this journal, that is. Following Jesus is a lifetime of commitment, but there's no better way to spend your life. Over the past several weeks, you've soaked yourself in God's Word, opened the lines of communication through prayer, made several sacrifices, taken many challenges, and chiseled away some of the rough edges of your life. In other words, you've been walking on the road behind Jesus. And chances are, that time you've spent following him—walking the same terrain, taking in the same nourishment, and standing in the same light—has made you look more like him. But there's always room to grow. Stay on the discipleship journey. Keep following Christ. It's the best way to live.

Appendix —

Spiritual Gifts Assessment
and ACTS Prayer Journal

SPIRITUAL GIFTS ASSESSMENT

After learning your wiring and how this fits within your leadership, it is vital to know exactly how Jesus has uniquely gifted you with special abilities to help in your kingdom work. Just as God equipped Moses with specific gifts to help him lead the Israelites, God has also equipped you with spiritual gifts to help you live out his mission in your life. This may be your first time ever identifying your unique spiritual gifts and it is exciting.

Your awareness of your gifts and your ability within your gifts will grow over time as you mature spiritually, continually striving to spend time with God and grow in your relationship with him. As you use your gifts, your confidence in them will grow.

This assessment was designed to help you identify your spiritual gifts. As with any assessment, your results will only be as accurate as the answers you give. Be sure to answer based on who you really are, not who you would like to be or who others think you ought to be.

Read the statements on the following pages carefully. Enter your ratings on the Response Sheet at the end of the assessment based on how well the statement describes you, using the following scale:

5   *Definitely Me*

4   *Very Much Like Me*

3   *Somewhat Like Me*

2   *Not Much Like Me*

1   *Definitely Not Me*

5-Definitely Me, 4-Very Much Like Me, 3-Somewhat Like Me, 2-Not Much Like Me, 1-Definitely Not Me

1.	I regularly encourage others to trust God, even when circumstances seem bleak.	5	4	3	2	1
2.	Others see me as caring and sensitive, and open up to me about their feelings.	5	4	3	2	1
3.	I willingly accept responsibility for leading groups that lack direction or motivation.	5	4	3	2	1
4.	I feel compelled to tell others about the inconsistencies I see and their impact.	5	4	3	2	1
5.	I seem better able than most people to sense when others are in need of a lift.	5	4	3	2	1
6.	I find it easy to engage non-believers in conversations about spiritual matters.	5	4	3	2	1
7.	I feel like a partner with the people and organizations I support financially.	5	4	3	2	1
8.	Others often ask me to research topics they want to understand more fully.	5	4	3	2	1
9.	I enjoy guiding and supporting individuals and groups seeking to learn and grow.	5	4	3	2	1
10.	Others see me as highly organized and look for my help in managing projects.	5	4	3	2	1
11.	I find that I am more adventurous and willing to take risks than most people.	5	4	3	2	1
12.	I enjoy analyzing difficult problems and discovering simple, practical solutions.	5	4	3	2	1
13.	I often seem to see matters of injustice or unfairness more clearly than other people.	5	4	3	2	1
14.	I enjoy working unrecognized behind the scenes to support the work of others.	5	4	3	2	1
15.	When I teach, I communicate clearly, and find it easy to engage people in learning.	5	4	3	2	1

5-Definitely Me, 4-Very Much Like Me, 3-Somewhat Like Me, 2-Not Much Like Me, 1-Definitely Not Me

16.	I am confident that God helps us to do great things when we trust him.	5	4	3	2	1
17.	I am easily moved by others' experience of heart-ache or suffering.	5	4	3	2	1
18.	I adjust my leadership style to work well with a variety of individuals or groups.	5	4	3	2	1
19.	I seem better able than most people to see the truth of what is really going on.	5	4	3	2	1
20.	Others see me as a positive, optimistic person who can make others feel good.	5	4	3	2	1
21.	I seem to be more concerned than most to share the gospel with non-believers.	5	4	3	2	1
22.	I feel deep satisfaction knowing my giving is making a real difference.	5	4	3	2	1
23.	I enjoy becoming more of an expert on a topic, and sharing my knowledge with others.	5	4	3	2	1
24.	I am more willing than other people to invest time in helping others grow as believers.	5	4	3	2	1
25.	I enjoy being relied upon to organize people and tasks to meet a goal.	5	4	3	2	1
26.	Others see me as a change agent and look to me to lead new undertakings.	5	4	3	2	1
27.	I frequently am able to see potential solutions to problems that others cannot.	5	4	3	2	1
28.	Others see me as a person of strong convictions and willing to speak out.	5	4	3	2	1
29.	I find fulfillment in faithfully performing tasks others see as unglamorous.	5	4	3	2	1
30.	I am confident in my ability to help others learn and apply knowledge and skills.	5	4	3	2	1

5-Definitely Me, 4-Very Much Like Me, 3-Somewhat Like Me, 2-Not Much Like Me, 1-Definitely Not Me

31.	I think I am more confident than most in trusting God, even in the hard times.	5	4	3	2	1
32.	I enjoy helping people that others may regard as undeserving or beyond help.	5	4	3	2	1
33.	I can successfully motivate, guide, and manage others to reach important goals.	5	4	3	2	1
34.	Others see me as insightful, a good judge of people and situations.	5	4	3	2	1
35.	People often seek me out when they are looking for affirmation or encouragement.	5	4	3	2	1
36.	Others see me as being confident in my faith, and ready and willing to share it.	5	4	3	2	1
37.	I give more generously than most people to church and other worthwhile causes.	5	4	3	2	1
38.	I share what I know confidently and clearly, helping others to understand.	5	4	3	2	1
39.	Others see me as a patient, supportive person who brings out the best in others.	5	4	3	2	1
40.	I am skilled at planning, organizing, and managing even complex projects.	5	4	3	2	1
41.	I am always looking for new experiences and love bringing about change.	5	4	3	2	1
42.	When asked to help solve a problem, people usually end up taking my advice.	5	4	3	2	1
43.	I feel a strong sense of responsibility to take a stand for what is right and true.	5	4	3	2	1
44.	I can see how my support with the little things helps others accomplish more.	5	4	3	2	1
45.	I believe I am more motivated to want to help others learn than most people.	5	4	3	2	1

5-*Definitely Me,* 4-*Very Much Like Me,* 3-*Somewhat Like Me,* 2-*Not Much Like Me,* 1-*Definitely Not Me*

46.	Others see me as having strong faith, able to provide spiritual encouragement.	5	4	3	2	1
47.	It makes me happy to bring comfort, hope, and joy to people facing difficulties	5	4	3	2	1
48.	I seem better able than most to help a group work together to achieve its goals.	5	4	3	2	1
49.	I always look below the surface to try to see the truth about people and situations.	5	4	3	2	1
50.	I am drawn to people who are confused or troubled, and try to cheer them up.	5	4	3	2	1
51.	In my relationships with non-believers, I regularly find ways to share my faith.	5	4	3	2	1
52.	It is important to manage my finances well so I can support causes I believe in.	5	4	3	2	1
53.	I like sharing knowledge that improves others' understanding and effectiveness.	5	4	3	2	1
54.	I willingly help others to grow in their faith and to improve their Christian walk.	5	4	3	2	1
55.	I enjoy helping a group to work efficiently and effectively to complete a project.	5	4	3	2	1
56.	I enjoy the challenge of trying new things, despite the unknowns or risks involved.	5	4	3	2	1
57.	I seem to see practical solutions to problems more readily than others.	5	4	3	2	1
58.	I am willing to speak out on matters of right and wrong even if unpopular.	5	4	3	2	1
59.	I seem more willing than most to pitch in wherever I can without being asked.	5	4	3	2	1
60.	Others see me as someone who can make difficult concepts easier to learn.	5	4	3	2	1

5-Definitely Me, 4-Very Much Like Me, 3-Somewhat Like Me, 2-Not Much Like Me, 1-Definitely Not Me

61.	I find it natural and easy to trust God to answer prayer for myself and others.	5 4 3 2 1
62.	I seem more compassionate than most, especially with people who are hurting.	5 4 3 2 1
63.	Others naturally look to me to lead, especially when facing big challenges.	5 4 3 2 1
64.	I can see through phoniness, deception, or error, usually before others are able to.	5 4 3 2 1
65.	I challenge people to look for and affirm the good in themselves and others.	5 4 3 2 1
66.	I like people to know I am a Christian and want them to ask me about my faith.	5 4 3 2 1
67.	I willingly contribute to projects needing my support or people in financial need.	5 4 3 2 1
68.	I think I am better than most people at gathering and sharing information.	5 4 3 2 1
69.	I see the things that hold people back and find ways to help them overcome.	5 4 3 2 1
70.	I think I am more organized than most, better able to manage complex tasks.	5 4 3 2 1
71.	My ability to adapt to new situations makes me comfortable with change.	5 4 3 2 1
72.	Others see me as having a lot of common sense and ask me for advice.	5 4 3 2 1
73.	I am comfortable challenging others to change their thoughts and actions.	5 4 3 2 1
74.	Others see me as always willing to pitch in and do even the smallest routine tasks.	5 4 3 2 1
75.	I enjoy preparing to teach—organizing and planning interesting learning experiences.	5 4 3 2 1

SCORING GUIDE

Response Sheet

Enter your responses in the appropriate boxes below. Place your score for question 1 in the box marked 1, and so on. After transferring all of your scores, add up the scores for each row and place the total in the column on the right.

TOTALS

1.	16.	31.	46.	61.	**1.**
2.	17.	32.	47.	62.	**2.**
3.	18.	33.	48.	63.	**3.**
4.	19.	34.	49.	64.	**4.**
5.	20.	35.	50.	65.	**5.**
6.	21.	36.	51.	66.	**6.**
7.	22.	37.	52.	67.	**7.**
8.	23.	38.	53.	68.	**8.**
9.	24.	39.	54.	69.	**9.**
10.	25.	40.	55.	70.	**10.**
11.	26.	41.	56.	71.	**11.**
12.	27.	42.	57.	72.	**12.**
13.	28.	43.	58.	73.	**13.**
14.	29.	44.	59.	74.	**14.**
15.	30.	45.	60.	75.	**15.**

Enter your totals from the *Response Sheet* in the appropriate spaces below.

	Gift	Description
1.	**Believing** *(Faith)*	Believing is a special God-given ability to trust God's will and act on it with an unwavering belief in God's concern, presence, and active participation.
2.	**Comforting** *(Mercy)*	Comforting is a special God-given ability to understand and come alongside people who are troubled or suffering, bringing them comfort, insight, and hope.
3.	**Directing** *(Leadership)*	Directing is a special God-given ability to instill vision, motivate, and guide people to work together effectively to achieve worthwhile goals.
4.	**Discerning** *(Discernment)*	Discerning is a special God-given ability to distinguish between truth and error, good and evil, and to show good judgment in matters involving character and relationships.
5.	**Encouraging** *(Exhortation)*	Encouraging is a special God-given ability to affirm, uplift, and restore confidence to individuals who are feeling discouraged or defeated.
6.	**Evangelizing** *(Evangelism)*	Evangelizing is a special God-given ability to effectively communicate the Good News of Jesus Christ to non-believers so they can respond and begin to grow in their faith.
7.	**Giving** *(Contributing)*	Giving is a special God-given ability to contribute cheerfully, generously, and regularly to the church and other important ministries, causes, and people in need.
8.	**Learning** *(Knowledge)*	Learning is a special God-given ability to gather, analyze, and share information appropriately with others, leading to greater understanding and insight.
9.	**Mentoring** *(Pastor/Shepherding)*	Mentoring is a special God-given ability to guide and support individuals or groups as they grow in their faith and in their capacity for ministry.
10.	**Organizing** *(Administration)*	Organizing is a special God-given ability to plan, organize tasks, and follow through so that complex projects are completed efficiently and effectively.
11.	**Pioneering** *(Apostleship)*	Pioneering is a special God-given ability to launch new ventures or lead change, confidently moving forward despite uncertainty or risk.
12.	**Problem-Solving** *(Wisdom)*	Problem-solving is a special God-given ability to provide practical advice that leads to timely, effective resolution of problems.
13.	**Speaking Out** *(Prophet)*	Speaking Out is a special God-given ability to declare God's truth boldly and publicly for the purpose of correction or instruction.
14.	**Supporting** *(Helps)*	Supporting is a special God-given ability to provide practical, behind-the-scenes help that frees others to accomplish more than they might otherwise be capable of achieving.
15.	**Teaching** *(Teacher)*	Teaching is a special God-given ability to organize and clearly communicate knowledge and skills to others, and to motivate them to master and apply what they are learning.

Review your scores from the previous page. Identify the two or three spiritual gifts that appear to be your strongest (your highest scores) and list these below.

My spiritual gifts may include:

_____

_____

_____

Next, take some time to learn more about these gifts. For each of your strongest gifts, review the gift summaries on the following pages. Take time to understand what each gift is and the unique contribution it enables you to make when you use it wisely. Think of examples where you have been able to use each gift effectively. How did it feel? What results did you achieve? Have you ever experienced any of the problems described in the Potential Pitfalls section of the summary?

BELIEVING

(Faith)

Basic Definition
Believing is a special God-given ability to trust God's will and act on it, with an unwavering belief in God's concern, presence, and active participation.

Unique Leadership Contribution
People with this gift trust God to answer prayer and encourage others to do so, confident in God's help, even in difficult times or in the face of opposition.

This Gift in Scripture
This gift is listed in 1 Corinthians 12:9 where it is usually translated as "faith" or "special faith."

This Gift in Use
People with this gift keep moving forward with confidence, undaunted by obstacles, encouraged by a deeply-rooted belief in God's unending faithfulness and constant care. They are also often the true prayer warriors of the church, lifting its needs to the Lord and seeking his will. When this gift is absent in the church, people can come to doubt God's goodness or his love and concern for his people.

This Gift in a Team
When the going gets tough, people with this gift step up and encourage the rest of the team to keep moving forward, trusting God for strength, guidance, and success.

Typical Strengths
People with this gift tend to be confident, optimistic, prayerful, and reliant on God. By declaring their own trust in God, they encourage others to move forward in faith too.

Potential Pitfalls
People with this gift can become weary and discouraged—or even angry and critical—when others do not share their confidence in God's concern or participation. Using this gift wisely involves remembering and reminding others of the many examples of God's faithfulness in the past, even during the bleakest times.

COMFORTING

(Mercy)

Basic Definition
Comforting is a special God-given ability to understand and come alongside people who are troubled or suffering, bringing them comfort, insight, and hope.

Unique Leadership Contribution
People with this gift patiently and compassionately help hurting people deal with painful experiences, even those whom others feel are undeserving or beyond help.

This Gift in Scripture
This gift is listed in Romans 12:8 where it is usually translated as "showing mercy" or "showing kindness."

This Gift in Use
People with this gift have a unique capacity for providing timely, practical support to hurting people, seemingly with endless patience, compassion, and joy in their hearts. They respond caringly to others' deepest needs, yet are able to look past their problems and circumstances and see their true worth as if through the eyes of God. When this gift is absent in the church, those who are truly needy will receive too little attention.

This Gift in a Team
In the life of any team there will be times when people need, more than anything, to be comforted by someone who comes alongside even as others pull back.

Typical Strengths
People with this gift tend to be caring, sensitive, and tolerant—natural burden bearers. They sense when people are down, and find ways to be there for them.

Potential Pitfalls
Sometimes, people with this gift become weighed down from carrying the burdens of others. Another problem may be that they may unintentionally enable others to avoid facing their difficulties or making hard choices. Using this gift wisely involves helping hurting people to deal with the underlying causes of their problems and not covering them up.

DIRECTING

(Leadership)

Basic Definition
Directing is a special God-given ability to instill vision, motivate, and guide people to work together effectively to achieve worthwhile goals.

Unique Leadership Contribution
People with this gift willingly take responsibility for directing groups, managing people, and resources effectively, and challenging others to perform at the highest level.

This Gift in Scripture
This gift is listed in Romans 12:8 where it is usually translated as "leadership" or "he who leads."

This Gift in Use
People with this gift help others aspire to and achieve lofty goals. They understand the importance of getting people to perform at their best, both individually and as a group. They relish the opportunity to be in a position of leadership where they can influence the performance of a group that is doing meaningful work. When this gift is absent in the church, people will find themselves falling well short of their potential.

This Gift in a Team
People with this gift are the natural leaders that all teams need to ensure that their efforts are guided by a vision worth pursuing and strategies worth implementing.

Typical Strengths
People with this gift tend to be goal-oriented, decisive, inspiring, and persuasive. They will tend to rise to the top in most groups, emerging naturally as the leader.

Potential Pitfalls
People with this gift need to avoid being over-confident in their own abilities and possibly pushing others away by their perceived arrogance or forcefulness. They can also get stuck in their own ways of doing things, becoming intolerant of others. Using this gift wisely involves building credibility, mutual trust, and support with followers.

DISCERNING

(Discernment)

Basic Definition
Discerning is a special God-given ability to distinguish between truth and error, good and evil, and to show good judgment in matters involving character and relationships.

Unique Leadership Contribution
People with this gift reliably distinguish between truth and error, good and evil, readily seeing through phoniness and deceit to perceive what is really going on.

This Gift in Scripture
This gift is listed in 1 Corinthians 12:10 where it is usually translated as "distinguishing between spirits" or "discerning of spirits."

This Gift in Use
People with this gift are unusually capable of recognizing inconsistencies in relationships, behavior, motives, teaching, and everyday practices. They quickly perceive the truth about these things, understand the potential consequences, and warn others to be on guard in order to avoid potentially risky situations. When this gift is absent in the church, people fall prey to false teaching or misguided leadership.

This Gift in a Team
At times, a team will find itself in situations where things are not really as they appear and must rely on the finely-tuned perception of someone with this gift to see the truth.

Typical Strengths
People with this gift are insightful, intuitive, and objective. They will often see things differently than others and will strongly defend their views if challenged.

Potential Pitfalls
People with this gift may need to work hard to avoid being seen by others as harsh and inflexible when sharing their insights, especially when their perceptions run counter to what others are thinking. Using this gift wisely involves taking the time to hear others' opinions, and to seek and share evidence that confirms what they think they are seeing.

ENCOURAGING

(Exhortation)

Basic Definition
Encouraging is a special God-given ability to affirm, uplift, and restore confidence to individuals who are feeling discouraged or defeated.

Unique Leadership Contribution
People with this gift sense the needs of others, particularly when they are feeling down, and provide much-appreciated reassurance and cheering up so they can carry on.

This Gift in Scripture
This gift is listed in Romans 12:8 where it is usually translated as "encouraging" or "exhortation."

This Gift in Use
People with this gift readily tune in to others who are in need of a boost. Typically positive and enthusiastic, they sense how others feel and what they need to do to encourage them. Sometimes they challenge or confront, and at other times they cheer up, applaud, or affirm. Whatever the situation, their goal is to help others feel better about themselves. When this gift is absent from a church, people can feel overwhelmed and give up.

This Gift in a Team
Every team needs at least one dedicated cheerleader, and that's a role people with this gift relish. When the going gets tough, they help people stay up and keep moving toward the goal.

Typical Strengths
People with this gift are usually sensitive, positive, and enthusiastic. They see the good in every person, the possibilities in every problem, and the light at the end of the tunnel.

Potential Pitfalls
At times, people with this gift can come across as too simplistic or idealistic. Others don't always appreciate their sunny disposition and unwavering optimism. Using this gift wisely involves acknowledging the reality of the circumstances people are facing and finding ways to offer not only encouragement, but also concrete, practical help.

EVANGELIZING

(Evangelism)

Basic Definition
Evangelizing is a special God-given ability to effectively communicate the Good News of Jesus Christ to non-believers so they can respond and begin to grow in their faith.

Unique Leadership Contribution
People with this gift find opportunities to build relationships with non-believers, comfortably sharing their faith, and inviting people to decide to follow Christ.

This Gift in Scripture
This gift is listed in Ephesians 4:11 where it is usually translated as "evangelists."

This Gift in Use
People with this gift communicate the Gospel with ease and effectiveness. They seek opportunities to build relationships with non-believers in order to demonstrate the good news of God's love in practical ways, and to get to know people better. This allows them to share their faith in ways that speak directly to the deepest needs of others. When this gift is absent from a church, people are reluctant to witness and outreach to non-believers will be ineffective.

This Gift in a Team
No matter what the primary focus of a team, there will be many opportunities to share the Gospel, and someone with this gift is most likely to recognize these opportunities and respond.

Typical Strengths
People with this gift tend to be social, secure in their faith, open, and candid. They willingly share their faith, doing so naturally and without much fear of rejection or ridicule.

Potential Pitfalls
At times, people with this gift will become discouraged when they are not seeing a response to their evangelistic efforts. Over time, they may become mechanical in their approach, or too aggressive, and turn off non-believers. Using this gift wisely means talking about your relationship with God, and inviting others to begin one of their own.

GIVING

(Contributing)

Basic Definition
Giving is a special God-given ability to contribute cheerfully, generously, and regularly to the church and other important ministries, causes, and people in need.

Unique Leadership Contribution
People with this gift manage their personal resources well, contributing as much as possible to people and organizations working to meet needs that are important to them.

This Gift in Scripture
This gift is listed in Romans 12:8 where it is usually translated as "contributing to the needs of others" or "he who gives."

This Gift in Use
People with this gift look for ways to increase their giving to the ministries, causes, and needy individuals they are most committed to supporting. They willingly limit spending on themselves and commit themselves to regular giving. They tend to see themselves as partners with those whose work they support and follow their work closely. When this gift is missing from the church, ministries will lack the resources required to fulfill their mission.

This Gift in a Team
People who are generous givers are often the best individuals to challenge others to do the same, making them a very effective agent for acquiring the resources the team needs.

Typical Strengths
People with this gift tend to be generous, conscientious, prudent, and resourceful. They look beyond their own needs, and see the benefit of meeting the needs of others.

Potential Pitfalls
Sometimes, people with this gift may be tempted to use their resources to pursue a pet project of their own. Or, they can feel unappreciated if their generosity is not adequately recognized. Using this gift wisely involves acknowledging that all we have comes from God and being grateful for the resources we have that we can use for His glory.

LEARNING

(Knowledge)

Basic Definition
Learning is a special God-given ability to gather, analyze, and share information appropriately with others, leading to greater understanding and insight.

Unique Leadership Contribution
People with this gift research topics of interest to themselves or others, organize their findings systematically, and share what they have learned with others.

This Gift in Scripture
This gift is listed in 1 Corinthians 12:8 where it is usually translated "message of knowledge," "word of knowledge," or "gift of special knowledge."

This Gift in Use
People with this gift are born researchers who love to accumulate and share information. Their unique interest leads them to keep exploring a subject to gain a deeper understanding and more useful information. They enjoy being invited to share their knowledge, helping others quickly gain deeper insight into important matters. When this gift is missing from the church, decisions and plans will be based on inadequate understanding and will eventually fail.

This Gift in a Team
Often people with this gift become a "walking library" of useful information on a wide range of topics crucial to the team's work, as well as the keeper of its learning history.

Typical Strengths
People with this gift tend to be inquisitive, analytical, and proud of their accumulated expertise, with a large appetite for acquiring and sharing information.

Potential Pitfalls
People with this gift need to remember that their latest discovery may not be as exciting to others as to them. They can also fall into the trap of being proud of what they know, even feeling superior to others as a result. The wise use of this gift involves learning to respond to others' self-identified needs for greater understanding in a given area.

MENTORING

(Pastor/Shepherding)

Basic Definition
Mentoring is a special God-given ability to guide and support individuals or groups as they grow in their faith and in their capacity for ministry.

Unique Leadership Contribution
People with this gift are committed to bringing out the best in others, patiently but firmly nurturing them in their development as whole persons, often on a long-term basis.

This Gift in Scripture
This gift is listed in Ephesians 4:11 where it is usually translated as "pastors."

This Gift in Use
People with this gift willingly accept responsibility for guiding and protecting people who they believe God has entrusted to their care. They identify others' strengths and limitations, and look for timely opportunities to challenge them to grow. Their long-term concern for people makes them highly trusted advisors and coaches. When this gift is missing from the church, people will remain weak in their faith and their Christian walk.

This Gift in a Team
Often people with this gift support a team by supporting its members in an ongoing process of personal and ministry development, both as individuals and as a group.

Typical Strengths
People with this gift tend to be nurturing, growth-minded, and discipleship-oriented. They will look for ways to maximize each person's growth and contribution.

Potential Pitfalls
People with this gift need to be careful about viewing certain people as projects. They may also have difficulty saying no, which can lead to burn-out. Using this gift wisely involves recognizing and maintaining appropriate boundaries, developing healthy relationships that avoid creating dependency between or among those involved.

ORGANIZING

(Administration)

Basic Definition
Organizing is a special God-given ability to plan, organize tasks, and follow through so that complex projects are completed efficiently and effectively.

Unique Leadership Contribution
People with this gift ensure the success of a project by clarifying goals, developing detailed plans, delegating tasks, monitoring performance, and managing follow-through.

This Gift in Scripture
This gift is listed in 1 Corinthians 12:28 where it is usually translated as "administration," "governments," or "those who can get others to work together."

This Gift in Use
People with this gift have the capacity to coordinate people, tasks, and resources even in very complex circumstances. Working within the context of the project's goals, they focus on both doing the right things and doing things right. They know how to bring order out of chaos in organizations, always able to see how everything fits together. When this gift is missing from the church, people will become frustrated by confusion, waste, and the inability to get things done.

This Gift in a Team
With so many tasks and people to manage, complexity is a fact of life for most teams. People with this gift develop the systems, processes, and plans to make it all work.

Typical Strengths
People with this gift tend to be highly-organized, thorough, clear-thinking, and conscientious. They are comfortable with detail and strive for order and harmony.

Potential Pitfalls
People with this gift must be careful not to frustrate other leaders who don't share their enthusiasm for thoroughness and detail. Also, when things aren't going well, they can sometimes seem to be "using people" simply to accomplish tasks. Using this gift wisely involves balancing task requirements and deadlines with people's needs and feelings.

PIONEERING

(Apostleship)

Basic Definition
Pioneering is a special God-given ability to launch new ventures or lead change, confidently moving forward despite uncertainty or risk.

Unique Leadership Contribution
People with this gift lead the way in spearheading change, testing out new ideas, or leading innovation, often producing breakthroughs in growth or effectiveness.

This Gift in Scripture
This gift is listed in 1 Corinthians 12:28 and Ephesians 4:11 where it is usually translated as "apostles."

This Gift in Use
People with this gift have little fear of the unknown, and an appetite for adventure and even risk. They look for opportunities for growth and change, seeking to move beyond the status quo. Where others get anxious, they get excited. Where others see obstacles, they see opportunities. They always look forward to the next challenge. When this gift is missing from the church, people will find it very difficult to bring about change or start something new.

This Gift in a Team
Even high performing teams can sometimes find themselves in a rut. It takes someone with this gift to stir things up, keep looking ahead, and push for much-needed changes.

Typical Strengths
People with this gift tend to be adventurous, risk-taking, adaptable, and confident. Being natural entrepreneurs, they have a make-it-happen approach to the future.

Potential Pitfalls
At times, people with this gift will move too quickly and get ahead of others. They may find themselves disconnected from the supporters they need, sometimes even alienating them. Using this gift wisely involves engaging others in creating a shared vision and in making plans to get there.

PROBLEM-SOLVING

(Wisdom)

Basic Definition
Problem-Solving is a special God-given ability to provide practical advice that leads to timely, effective resolution of problems.

Unique Leadership Contribution
People with this gift can often identify simple, practical solutions to problems, helping others find ways to get unstuck and confidently move forward toward their goals.

This Gift in Scripture
This gift is listed in 1 Corinthians 12:8 where it is usually translated as "message of wisdom," "word of wisdom," or "the ability to give wise advice."

This Gift in Use
People with this gift see solutions where others may only see roadblocks. They seem to be able to cut through confusion and conflict and see how to overcome obstacles. They are good at figuring out the best action to take in a given situation. Blessed with an uncommon amount of common sense, they offer practical advice that others willingly follow. When this gift is missing from the church, people may repeat past mistakes or continue doing things the hard way.

This Gift in a Team
Every team runs into problems and needs someone who can offer practical advice to get the team back on track as well as helping the team avoid getting bogged down in the first place.

Typical Strengths
People with this gift will tend to be logical, sensible, observant, and highly practical. They will see options others miss and carefully choose the most effective way forward.

Potential Pitfalls
People with this gift may be tempted to hold back from sharing their insights until someone invites them to do so, perhaps because they have learned that others are not always open to advice. Using this gift wisely involves learning how to share important insights and suggestions in ways that others can understand and embrace them.

SPEAKING OUT

(Prophet)

Basic Definition
Speaking Out is a special God-given ability to declare God's truth boldly and publicly for the purpose of correction or instruction.

Unique Leadership Contribution
People with this gift challenge others to change their behavior by speaking out clearly and convincingly about right and wrong, even where it may be unpopular.

This Gift in Scripture
This gift is listed in Romans 12:6; 1 Corinthians 12:10, 28; and Ephesians 4:11 where it is usually translated as "prophesying," "prophets," or "ability to prophesy."

This Gift in Use
People with this gift are especially attuned both to God's principles and to what is really going on in the world. They look for the right time and place to share what they feel must be said to influence others. They tend to see issues that others fail to see and feel compelled to speak out. When this gift is missing from the church, people can lose touch with God's heart and his will.

This Gift in a Team
Often people with this gift support a team by serving as a kind of "moral compass," challenging others to live up to biblical standards of right and wrong.

Typical Strengths
People with this gift will tend to be individualistic, opinionated, outspoken, and determined. They will see situations and issues in very clear, black-and-white terms.

Potential Pitfalls
At times, people with this gift will be difficult to be around because of their strong need to speak out, which may be perceived as overly judgmental and critical of others. Using this gift wisely involves being compassionate toward others and having a genuine desire to motivate others to change rather than a need simply to point out where they are wrong.

SUPPORTING

(Helps)

Basic Definition
Supporting is a special God-given ability to provide practical, behind-the-scenes help that frees others to accomplish more than they might otherwise be capable of achieving.

Unique Leadership Contribution
People with this gift usually like to work behind the scenes, supporting the work of others, cheerfully finding and doing small things that need doing, often without being asked.

This Gift in Scripture
This gift is listed in Romans 12:7 and 1 Corinthians 12:28 where it is usually translated as "helps," "serving," "ministry," "forms of assistance," or "those able to help others."

This Gift in Use
People with this gift take pride in doing well the seemingly small tasks others sometimes consider mundane or routine. They appreciate how their faithful assistance with these tasks pays off by freeing others to focus their attention on "higher level" tasks and enables them to use their gifts more fully. When this gift is missing from the church, leaders can become bogged down by details or worn out from trying to do everything alone.

This Gift in a Team
No one gets to do the glamorous work all of the time, but those with this gift willingly take on the more routine tasks, making it possible for high-performing teams to excel.

Typical Strengths
People with this gift tend to be flexible, easy-going, dependable, and humble. They take pride in serving others faithfully without concern for recognition or honor.

Potential Pitfalls
People with this gift often find it difficult to say no, causing them to over-commit, which leads to a loss of balance in their lives. Some also come to depend on what they do for others for their self-worth. Using this gift wisely involves recognizing that God values people for who they are, not what they do, and by maintaining a healthy, balanced life.

TEACHING

(Teacher)

Basic Definition
Teaching is a special God-given ability to organize and clearly communicate knowledge and skills to others, and to motivate them to master and apply what they are learning.

Unique Leadership Contribution
People with this gift identify the knowledge and skills others need to learn, and use creative approaches to help them learn willingly and effectively.

This Gift in Scripture
This gift is listed in Romans 12:7; 1 Corinthians 12:28; and Ephesians 4:11 where it is usually translated as "teaching" or "teacher."

This Gift in Use
People with this gift focus on helping others develop their knowledge and skill, including their knowledge of Christian principles. They begin by understanding the learning needs of others, and then look for teachable moments to engage people in creative, enjoyable learning activities that lead to knowledge and skill improvement. When this gift is missing from the church, people will not grow in depth of faith or capacity for ministry.

This Gift in a Team
Often people with this gift have the best feel for the strengths and limitations of the team. They often can tell what others need to learn and how to help them learn it.

Typical Strengths
People with this gift will usually be skilled at organizing ideas, creative, and enthusiastic. They have a special knack for making difficult concepts easier to learn.

Potential Pitfalls
The most common shortcoming of people with this gift is their tendency to over-teach, presenting too much content and not enough opportunity for reflection, review, and experimenting with application. Using this gift wisely involves continually "checking in" with the learners and adjusting to their motivation, pace, and learning style.

Use this ACTS prayer model each time you pray this week:

1. Adoration: Praise God for who he is. What fact or characteristic about God makes you glad?

2. Confession: Humble yourself. If Jesus took a tour of your heart right now, what would he find?

3. Thanksgiving: Be grateful. What happened in your life today that you can thank God for?

4. Supplication: Tell God your needs. Where do you need him to work in your life?

5. Listen: What is God saying to you? Think about things others have told you, past experiences, familiar Bible passages, and even the Holy Spirit's tugging on your heart. God speaks through these things.

Use this ACTS prayer model each time you pray this week:

1. Adoration: Praise God for who he is. What fact or characteristic about God makes you glad?

2. Confession: Humble yourself. If Jesus took a tour of your heart right now, what would he find?

3. Thanksgiving: Be grateful. What happened in your life today that you can thank God for?

4. Supplication: Tell God your needs. Where do you need him to work in your life?

5. Listen: What is God saying to you? Think about things others have told you, past experiences, familiar Bible passages, and even the Holy Spirit's tugging on your heart. God speaks through these things.

Use this ACTS prayer model each time you pray this week:

1. Adoration: Praise God for who he is. What **fact or characteristic** about God makes you glad?

2. Confession: Humble yourself. If Jesus took a **tour of your heart** right now, what would he find?

3. Thanksgiving: Be grateful. What happened **in your life today that** you can thank God for?

4. Supplication: Tell God your needs. Where **do you need him to work in** your life?

5. Listen: What is God saying to you? Think about **things others have** told you, past experiences, familiar Bible passages, and even the Holy Spirit's tugging on your heart. God speaks through these things.

Use this ACTS prayer model each time you pray this week:

1. Adoration: Praise God for who he is. What fact or characteristic about God makes you glad?

2. Confession: Humble yourself. If Jesus took a tour of your heart right now, what would he find?

3. Thanksgiving: Be grateful. What happened in your life today that you can thank God for?

4. Supplication: Tell God your needs. Where do you need him to work in your life?

5. Listen: What is God saying to you? Think about things others have told you, past experiences, familiar Bible passages, and even the Holy Spirit's tugging on your heart. God speaks through these things.

Use this ACTS prayer model each time you pray this week:

1. Adoration: Praise God for who he is. What **fact or characteristic** about God makes you glad?

2. Confession: Humble yourself. If Jesus took a **tour of your heart** right now, what would he find?

3. Thanksgiving: Be grateful. What happened in your life today that you can thank God for?

4. Supplication: Tell God your needs. Where **do you need him to work in** your life?

5. Listen: What is God saying to you? Think about things others have told you, past experiences, familiar Bible passages, and even the Holy Spirit's tugging on your heart. God speaks through these things.

ENDNOTES

[1]Calvin, John. *Institutes of the Christian Religion*. Grand Rapids, MI: William B. Eerdmans Pub. Co, 1983.

[2]Nouwen, Henri J. M. *Here and Now: Living in the Spirit with Guide for Reflection*. New York: Crossroad, 2003.

[3]Jobs, Steve. Commencement Speech, Stanford University, Stanford, 2005.

[4]Packer, J. I. *Knowing God*. London: Hodder & Stoughton, 2013.

[5]Manning, Brennan. *Ruthless Trust: The Ragamuffin's Path to God*. London: SPCK, 2002.

[6]Buechner, Frederick, and Brian D. McLaren. *Secrets in the Dark: A Life in Sermons*. New York: HarperOne, 2007.

[7]Wright, N T. *Surprised by Hope: Rethinking Heaven, the Resurrection, and the Mission of the Church*. New York: HarperOne, 2014.

[8]Spurgeon, Charles. "She Was Not Hid." *The Complete Works of C. H. Spurgeon, Volume 34: Sermons 2001-2061*. Harrington: Delmarva Publications, Inc., 2015.

[9]Galli, Mark. *Chaos and Grace: Discovering the Liberating Work of the Holy Spirit*. Grand Rapids, Mich: Baker Books, 2011.

[10]Warren, Richard. *The Purpose of Christmas*. New York: Howard Books, 2008.

[11] "Billy Graham." BrainyQuote.com. Xplore Inc, 2017. 27 March 2017. https://www.brainyquote.com/quotes/quotes/b/billygraha401823.html.

[12]"Brennan Manning." BrainyQuote.com. Xplore Inc, 2017. 24 March 2017. https://www.brainyquote.com/quotes/quotes/b/brennanman531776.html.

[13]Lewis, C S. *The Complete C.S. Lewis Signature Classics*. San Francisco, CA: HarperSanFrancisco, 2007.

[14]Vonnegut, Kurt. "Thoughts of a Free Thinker" Commencement Address, Hobart and William Smith Colleges, Geneva, 1974.

Check out these other journals made just for you:
(Go to Leadertreks.org for more info.)

LeaderTreks has summer internships!

If you are in college you can join a LeaderTreks staff member to lead missions or wilderness trips. Learn more about our internship program at Leadertreks.org/jobs.

Making Disciples. Developing Leaders.

leadertreks.org 877-502-0699